Dave —
To a great friend and
fellow sports enthusiast.
I always enjoy our road trips
to various game sites (eg Morgantown,
Buffalo, Olean).
   May God continue to bless
you and your family. Believe
in the power of prayer.
      Chuck
      (Phil 4:6,7)
      (1 Thess 5:17)

A Book of Prayers:
To the Heavens from the Stars

by
Chuck Spinner

authorHOUSE®

AuthorHouse™
1663 Liberty Drive, Suite 200
Bloomington, IN 47403
www.authorhouse.com
Phone: 1-800-839-8640

First published by AuthorHouse 1/8/2008

ISBN: 978-1-4343-3265-3 (sc)

Library of Congress Control Number: 2007910172

Printed in the United States of America
Bloomington, Indiana

This book is printed on acid-free paper.

The Scripture quotations contained herein are from the New Revised Standard Version Bible, copyright @ 1989 by the Division of Christian Education of the National Council of the Churches of Christ in the U.S.A., and are used by permission. All rights reserved.

The Scripture quotations indicated above refer to all instances when chapters and verses alone were listed by celebrities. The author has printed untouched any bible passage that was sent in that was directly quoted by a celebrity. These passages come from a number of different biblical translations.

For the *Lord's Prayer*, the author has used the English translation found in the 1662 Anglican Book of Common Prayer (BCP).

"DENNIS THE MENACE used by permission of Hank Ketcham Enterprises and North America Syndicate."

Prayer quotes in the last section were garnered from a variety of web site sources.

Acknowledgements

Thanks to my very talented nephew, JD Spinner, for creating the fantastic cover for this book. My deep gratitude extends also to my great friend, Doug Dieken, who wrote such a wonderful Foreword. Thanks to my friend and former teaching colleague Rosemary Merchant for helping with proofreading. The following people are especially appreciated for encouraging me in this project: Barb Jender, Tabitha Butler, Alex Adams, Al Siebert, Al Toenjes, the Hogan's Hut Breakfast Bunch, Craig Phillips, Eileen Clegg, Fred Tavakovi, Dave Howard, Andrew Silvernail and most especially Reverend Monsignor Joseph M. Dowdell. Steve Spinner helped obtain a response from John McVay. Gini Archer was instrumental in helping me acquire the favorite prayers of several celebrities. My subscription to startiger.com (suggested by Drew Sawyer) aided greatly in locating addresses for celebrities. I am indebted to AuthorHouse for providing me the avenue and the assistance that enabled me to put this work into print. Thanks to my siblings John, Bob, and Mary Lou and their families for their interest and support in this endeavor. And, finally, I don't think I would have persevered with this book of prayers had it not been for the loving concern from my four good guys: Scott and Ellen and Caleb and Joshua.

Table of Contents

Acknowledgements..v

Foreword by Doug Dieken..xi

Dedication xiv

Prayer xviii

Scott Alexander – Musician...1

Kim Alexis – Model 3

Steve Alford – Basketball player and coach 5

June Allyson – Actress 6

Leah O'Brien-Amico – Three time Olympic gold medalist, softball 9

Patty Berg – Legendary women's golf champion 10

Yogi Berra – Great New York Yankee Catcher.............12

Bobby Bowden – FSU football coach 14

Dan Britton – Senior VP of ministries for FCA...........16

John Brockington – Fullback: Ohio State and Green Bay..........18

Lane Brody – Singer/songwriter/actress 20

Betty Buckley – Broadway star 21

Dyan Cannon– Movie/TV Actress 23

Kristen Chenoweth – Actress/singer 24

Tara Dawn Holland Christensen – Miss America 1997 26

Mario Cuomo – Former Governor of New York...........31

Clive Cussler – Author 32

Ann B. Davis – "Alice" on the Brady Bunch 34

Pete Dawkins – Army Heisman Trophy winner 35

Laraine Day – Movie Actress 37

Dom DeLuise – Movie/TV Actor..................................38

Phyllis Diller – Comedienne 39

Vince Dooley – Georgia football coach and AD 41

Dave Dravecky – Baseball Pitcher 42

Denise Dufala – Cleveland news anchor....................................45

Father Virgil Elizondo – Theology professor, Notre Dame........46

Carl Erskine – Dodgers pitcher 48

Mike Eruzione – Captain of the 1984 gold medal hockey team.49

Gerry Faust – Notre Dame and Akron University football
coach..51

General Tommy Franks – U.S. general/Iraqi War 54

Father Joseph Girzone – Author of "Joshua" series....................56

Archie Griffin – Only two-time Heisman Trophy winner 58

Karolyn Grimes – Played "Zuzu" in *It's a Wonderful Life* 60

Ioan Gruffudd – Welsh actor..63

Janet Guthrie – First Woman driver in the Indy 500 65

Mike Hargrove – Baseball player/manager................................67

Brian Harper – Baseball catcher..69

Mother Dolores Hart – Movie star; Mother Superior 71

Ernie Harwell – Announcer for the Detroit Tigers 72

Father Edward Hays – Religious author/specialty is prayer........74

Michael Heaton – Columnist for the *Cleveland Plain Dealer* 75

Bunny Hoest – Cartoonist ("Lockhorns") 77

Lou Holtz – ND and South Carolina football coach 78

Victoria Jackson – Commedienne (*Saturday Night Live*)...........80

Dr. William N. Jackson – Pastor and famous preacher 82

Ann Jillian – Actress 84

Shirley Mae Jones – Actress (Movie/Broadway/TV)..................85

Al Kaline – Hall of Fame baseball player/Detroit Tigers 87

Bil Keane – *Family Circus* cartoonist..88

Rex Kern – Quarterback – The Ohio State University 90

Nancy Lopez Knight – Hall of Fame women's golfer 93

Don Larsen – Pitched World Series perfect game 94

Joan Leslie – Movie actress 96

Tom Lester – Eb Dawson on *Green Acres* 98

Evangeline Lilly – One of the stars of TV show *Lost* 100

Art Linkletter – Entertainer (*House Party*) 101

Dick Locher – Cartoonist ("Dick Tracy") 102

Trini Lopez – Singer/actor..104

Susie Luchsinger – Country/gospel singer 106

Johnny Lujack – Heisman Trophy QB for Notre Dame 107

Katherine MacGregor – Harriet Olsen on *Little House on the Prairie* 109

Melissa Manchester – Singer/songwriter................................111

Rose Marie – Comedienne (*Dick Van Dyke Show*) 112

Jack Marschall – Cleveland News Anchor................................113

Coach Jack McKeon – Two-time MBL Coach of the Year 115

Gilbert "Gil" James McDougald – New York Yankee baseball player 117

Scott McGregor – Baltimore Oriole pitcher 119

John McVay – VP/GM of San Francisco 49ers........................122

Patrice Munsel – Opera singer..123

Queen Noor – Queen of Jordan 124

John Jordan "Buck" O'Neil – Negro League baseball player 126

Tom Osborne – Nebraska football coach/U.S. Representative/ AD 128

Charles Osgood – Commentator..129

Andy Pafko – Chicago Cubs Baseball player............................132

Patti Page – Singer..134

Walter William "Billy" Pierce – Chicago White Sox pitcher 135

A. James Quinn – Auxiliary Bishop of Cleveland, Ohio 137

Mary Lou Retton – Olympic gold medal gynmast...................139

Bobby Richardson – New York Yankee baseball player 140

Daniel "Rudy" Ruettiger – Notre Dame football walk-on;
Rudy 142

Sam Rutigliano – Coach: Browns, Liberty University, NFL
Euro 144

Tim Salmon – Anaheim Angels baseball player.......................146

Joan Benoit Samuelson – Olympic gold medalist/marathon 148

Cael Sanderson – Four-time NCAA wrestling champ.............149

Stephen Schwartz – Broadway producer..................................152

General H. Norman Schwarzkopf – General/Operation Desert
Storm 154

Paul Scofield – Oscar winner/*A Man for all Seasons* 156

Herb Score – Cleveland Indians pitcher/announcer..................157

George Beverly Shea – Tenor/singer with Billy Graham Crusade.....159

Martin Sheen – Actor/activist...161

Senator Alan K. Simpson – U.S. Senator from Wyoming........163

Scott Simpson – U.S. Open golf champion..............................165

Coach Dean Smith – U. of North Carolina basketball coach...168

Ellen Pasturzak Spinner – Miss Ohio 1996.............................170

Scott Lee Spinner – Dad Vail rowing champion 172

Dana Summers – Political cartoonist/*Orlando Sentinel* 174

Jim Sundberg – Baseball player..176

Steve Tasker – Seven-times selected to NFL Pro Bowl.............178

Bobby Thomson – Hit most famous home run in history 179

Lonnie Melvin "Mel" Tillis – Singer/actor..............................181

Jacquelyn Mayer Townsend – Miss America 1963 183

Fred Travalena – Singer/impersonator 185

Jim Tressel – Ohio State football coach..................................188

Virgil "Fire" Trucks – Detroit Tigers pitcher.........................189

Bishop Desmond Mpilo Tutu – Nobel Peace Prize recipient....191

Marilyn Van Derbur – Miss America 1958............................192

Richard J. "Dick" Vitale – Sports announcer.........................194

Senator George Victor Voinovich – U.S. Senator from Ohio...196

Mort Walker – Cartoonist ("Beetle Bailey")..........................198

Rusty Wallace – Race car driver...200

Kurt Warner – Two-time NFL MVP.....................................202

Thelma Wells – One of leaders of Women of Faith................205

Father Robert Welsh, SJ – President/Cleveland St. Ignatius
High School..208

Dr. Robert White – Cleveland neurosurgeon.........................210

Dr. Walter Wink – Minister, professor, author......................211

John Wooden – Legendary UCLA basketball coach 213

Danny Wuerffel – Heisman Trophy winner/U. of Florida 216

Norma Larsen Zimmer – "Champagne Lady"/*The Lawrence
Welk Show* 218

Prayer Quotations 221

Foreword
by Doug Dieken

When I started playing for the Cleveland Browns in the early 1970s, I had a teammate by the name of Gene Hickerson from the South. Gene had a saying: "He's good people." The translation was that the person had the qualities that you wanted to find in a person, to describe how they conducted themselves.

In the late '70s, I got introduced to a history teacher at Normandy High School on Cleveland's South Side. His name was Chuck Spinner. I've known Chuck now for nearly thirty years and I've learned that there is a level above "He's good people." Chuck Spinner? "He's *great* people."

Before I met Chuck, he had graduated from Conception Seminary College. He eventually left his seminary studies and married the love of his life, Patrice. Their marriage has had thirty-seven great years and provided them with a son, Scott, who is the son you want your son to grow up to be in life. Scott and his wife, Ellen, a former Miss Ohio, have provided Chuck and Patrice with two fine grandsons, Caleb and Joshua.

In Webster's Dictionary under "family," I would never be surprised if they have a picture of the Spinner clan. Patrice, a former beautician, was my barber in the basement of their home. Scott was my pigeon for any new video game that was just released.

In the world of professional sports, people often want to have a piece of you for who you are and what you do in life. This is why I always felt comfortable in the Spinners' house. They were your friends because of what you were about in life. Your occupation was just your job and the most important thing about you was your friendship.

Chuck had some unusual interests that always amazed and amused me. My idea of a fun afternoon had never been studying cemeteries, tombstones, and grave markings. However, I always found Chuck's knowledge to be impressive and interesting. When Chuck changed schools and went to Shaker Heights High School, I went over to observe one of his classes to observe him and his guest lecturer. The passion he put into his teaching profession was quite obvious; I've never seem him do anything that wasn't 100 percent effort. In fact, when I was asked to make a Memorial Day speech in Bay Village, Ohio, I asked Chuck for some help. I not only got help, I got a speech worthy of a politician addressing Congress.

It came as no surprise that after Chuck retired from teaching and to a cottage home on Lake Chautauqua, New York, his part-time job giving tours of the lake wouldn't be enough to fill his plate.

Chuck's new passion was finding spiritual prayers that were the backbone of many notable, successful people. He found that the prayers that were sent to him were part of these people's foundation. His book, *To the Heavens from the Stars*, has over 100 favorite prayers from Oscar winners, Heisman Trophy winners, Olympic Gold medalists, four-star generals, and a Nobel Peace Prize recipient. They even include one country's monarch, former Miss Americas, and other notable celebrities and athletes.

The book gives you a chance to know what these people that you know for their achievements in life are also about in their spiritual formation. In a world where headlines are often made by famous people who have done something bad, the book *To the Heavens from the Stars* presents famous people who are role models for their beliefs as well as their worldly achievements.

Chuck Spinner is what's good about life. He has written this book to share what's good about others in their life that we know only from a distance. Chuck is "great people" and his book is a "great read."

About Doug Dieken:

Doug played fourteen years as offensive tackle for the Cleveland Browns and now is enjoying his twentieth year as radio color commentator for his former team.

Dedication

I was born and raised in what was then the sleepy little town of Naperville, Illinois—population 6,000. Naperville has long ago transformed its farmland into a suburban giant that now has approximately 145,000 residents. Like my two older brothers, John and Bob, I determined the seasons by baseball, basketball, and football, rather than summer, fall, winter, and spring.

April 16, 1961 is a day that will live tragically in my heart forever. It was the day that my father died in his sleep. He was fifty years old. I was fourteen. From my perspective, my dad was an older man. Now that I am over sixty years old myself, I realize just how young my father was at the time of his death. My dad and mom did not get to celebrate their twenty-fifth wedding anniversary. My dad did not live to see any of his grandchildren. So, each day, I am grateful for the new day the Lord has given to me. I thank God for thirty-seven wonderful years of marriage and for two exceptional grandchildren.

My father lived an exemplary life. He was raised on a farm and then worked for twenty-five years at the Kroehler Furniture Factory. Then, he and his brother Bill bought a package liquor store that they operated for several years before my dad's death. My dad was a people person. All classes of people in all manner of dress were present at his funeral service. I think few of those people knew what a prayerful person my father was. Every night, he would go off by himself and say the rosary.

My mother was one of twelve children. Two of those kids went on to enter the religious life. My parents made sure that their five children attended weekly church services, went to parochial grade school, and made God a priority in their lives. It is not surprising that thoughts of a religious vocation were encouraged for John and Louise's children.

After my dad died, I entered the seminary. I spent my last three years of high school at Servite Seminary in Hillside, Illinois. Then I graduated from Conception College Seminary, about 100 miles north of Kansas City, Missouri.

During the summer of 2003, I revisited Conception Seminary for my thirty-fifth college class reunion. I was very impressed with the physical plant (i.e., the care of the grounds, the building construction, and especially with the remodeled Basilica). As much as I was pleased with those material appearances, I was even more taken with the presence, poise, and prayer life of the seminarians that I met. I joined the students for morning and evening prayers (Lauds and Vespers). Their melodic, slowly paced recitation of the psalms established a contemplative mood that encouraged the seminarians to focus on what was being read and reflected upon.

My sister, Jean, died three years after my father's death. I was a senior in high school at the minor seminary. My sister had gone in for a routine physical to a young doctor who was just starting out upon his career. After her physical exam, Jean asked the young physician if he thought that the small veins in her legs might in time develop into varicose veins like her mother's. The doctor had her return to his office the following week, during which time he removed the veins in question. The procedure dislodged a blood clot that ultimately led to her death two days later.

Through the deaths of her husband and daughter, my mother was a rock of strength. She continued to diligently raise her remaining four children and saw that all four received a college education. My mother always reminded her children that a person's character is determined by the acceptance of both the misfortunes as well as the benevolences that might come that person's way.

I learned the value and power of prayer from the deaths of my father and my sister. I began to pray to my God through my father and my sister, and I believe that I received special gifts through their intercession on my behalf.

After I graduated from college, I left my seminary studies and began a thirty-three-year teaching career in the Cleveland, Ohio area. In 1970, I married Patrice Supik. My wife and I celebrated our thirty-seventh wedding anniversary on August 1, 2007. I believe that our marriage has been strengthened by the challenges that my wife and I have had to face along the way. Two days before Christmas in 1995, we received a phone call at one in the morning. My wife answered the phone and I shuddered when I heard her ask, "Is he still alive?" Our only son, Scott, had been hit head-on by a drunk driver who had passed out at the wheel. The driver had no license, no insurance, and had twenty-six previous driving violations! The next several years of our life found us dealing with operations, medical bills, legal problems, and court cases. Scott ultimately recovered nearly 100 percent.

During the past fifteen years, my wife Patrice has been beset with a number of physical problems that would also test our will and our spirit. During this time, she has had two rotator cuff surgeries. She has had severe back problems that necessitated the placement of two rods and crossover brackets that were inserted into her spinal column. In the summer of 2003, she was diagnosed with breast cancer, and the next year, she had a cancerous right kidney removed. Patrice's physical challenges continued in 2005 as she underwent two operations, one for a total knee replacement and another for a ruptured appendix. In 2006, Patrice had a total hysterectomy when some irregularities were discovered on her ovaries.

People who meet my wife, like those who knew my mother, would never know that these two women were ever beset with any physical problems or emotional stress. My wife is a warrior who has fought cancer twice successfully. She—not unlike my mother—trusts in the power of prayer. She tells people that her bouts with cancer were too much for her to deal with, so she handed those problems over to the Lord.

As I wrote this book I looked both to the past and to the future. I often received inspiration from the memory of my father, John, and my sister, Jean. But, I also looked upon this endeavor as a gift to the future as represented by our two grandsons, Caleb and Joshua. What I hope that this book ultimately presents to its readers is the resolve of my mother and my wife: that no matter what problems or difficulties might await us in life, they can be made easier or at least more bearable through the power of prayer. My mother, Louise Rechenmacher Spinner, and my wife, Patrice Supik Spinner, are my own personal heroes and/or celebrities, and it is to these two women that I have dedicated my efforts.

Prayer

"…but in everything by prayer and supplication with thanksgiving let your requests be made known to God. And the peace of God, which surpasses all understanding, will guard your hearts and your minds…" (Philippians 4:6,7)

Prayer has always been a part of my life. Not always as much as it should be, or in the form it is now, or, for that matter, in the form I hope it will become. I have gone through periods of time in my life when everything else seemed more important, and at those times, some aspects of prayer got pushed to the side.

I was always taught that there are four purposes for prayer: thanksgiving, adoration, petition, and satisfaction for one's sins.

<u>THANKSGIVING</u>: Of the four purposes of prayer mentioned above, the most neglected are thanksgiving, adoration, and satisfaction for one's sins. Isn't it interesting that our country sets aside just one day for Thanksgiving? And isn't it more ironic that during this one day more time by far is devoted to preparing meals and watching parades and football games than in giving thanks? I don't think I would be wrong to say that even during this one day

out of the year, in many homes no "thanksgiving" whatsoever is given during the holiday.

How we all like a good "pat on the back," an acknowledgement that we have worth and are loved. As children of a loving God, it makes sense for us to thank our God for all the many blessings we receive daily. When things are going well for us, this might seem like an easy thing to do. It really is not. As many other teachers can attest, when students receive an "A" or a "B" grade on a report card, most often they will say that "I earned that grade." When students receive a "D" or and "F" grade, most often they will say that "the teacher gave me that grade." And so it is, I believe, with our relationship with our God. When things are going well, it is easy for us to say that our success was due entirely to our own good efforts. When more difficult times confront us, we wonder how our God could bring such trials into our lives.

My father died when I was a freshman in high school. He was fifty years old. I am now over sixty and consider each day of my life that I have lived—especially those past the age of fifty—to be a gift from God. So each morning, the first prayer I say is one of thanksgiving for the gift of life and for the wonderful family God has blessed me with: my wife, Patrice; my son, Scott, and his wife, Ellen; and our grandkids, Caleb and Joshua. Then I simply say "Good morning, dear Jesus. Everything I do today and every day, I do for you. Please help me to do well." This, in effect, commits everything I do during the day as a prayer to God.

We are living in a very materialistic society. We never want for something to want. And our media is there to help us decide what and how much to covet. It's pretty easy to say "thank you" at a birthday or a holiday for something that we probably will get tired of in a ridiculously short period of time. We can give thanks for the treadmill we won't use, the coat that we won't long wear because it is too soon out of fashion, even the car that loses its appeal when it gets nicks and scratches along with mounting miles. Why then is it that we forget to express our thanks for a God who has provided us with marvels beyond comprehension? We have a universe whose wonders will forever keep photographers, scientists, artists, and poets occupied trying to examine it, quantify it, and capture it in some form or fashion. If we are impressed with the work of a watchmaker, how much more should we appreciate the work of a world maker!

And what can we give our Lord for all he has given us? I think Christina G. Rossetti said it best in this short poem:

> *"What can I give Him poor as I am?*
> *If I were a shepherd, I would give Him a lamb.*
> *If I were a wise man, I would do my part, --*
> *But what can I give Him,*
> *Give my heart."*

Any grandparent will agree with Rossetti that the best gift grandchildren can give their grandparents (and vice versa) is the gift of time, the gift of concern, and the gift of love.

ADORATION: My uncle Leroy was a judge, and as such, he could perform marriage ceremonies. I remember particularly one Saturday evening when he was eating dinner with our family. He received a phone call from a young couple who just in the last couple of days had met, got their marriage license, and now wanted to get married that evening. My uncle refused their request and asked that they call his office on Monday. I was very young at the time and at first felt that my uncle should have acquiesced to the lovers' wishes. Then my uncle patiently explained to me that from his experience, he would be very surprised if the couple still wanted to be married on Monday. He said that because the couple did not present any extenuating circumstances, he felt the call was to persuade one of the partners to engage in weekend sex, rather than to commit to lifelong marriage. "How could this couple love and adore each other?" my uncle questioned me. "They don't even know each other!"

In order to really love and adore each other, a couple must know each other as completely as possible. And to love our God, it seems equally important to talk with Him through prayer, to learn about Him through the inspired words of the Bible, and to receive Him into our hearts through Communion.

It is always amazing to me how our society adores its celebrities. This perception is what led me to believe that the participation of well-known personalities would certainly draw or attract the public to this book on prayer. The not-so-famous people go to any lengths to find out any variety of intricate, personal details about famous people. In their attempts to have some tie-in to a celebrity, a person might view relics, collect autographs, seek physical contact, or take a picture. Would that the great mass of people would show that same amount of enthusiasm in the adoration of our most precious celebrity, our Lord God! Every year, millions of fans go wild at sporting events throughout the world in order to cheer their favorite team to win a game or championship of some sort. Would that we would mount that same enthusiasm for the God who has assured us of the greatest reward imaginable—life everlasting! And just as we train to win a game, shouldn't we train as hard or harder for this greater reward? St. Paul said it best in his letter to the Corinthians (9:24-25) when he instructed,

> "Do you not know that in a race all the runners run,
> but only one gets the prize? Run in such a way as to
> get the prize. Everyone who goes into the games goes
> into strict training. They do it to get a crown that

will not last; but we do it to get a crown that will last forever."

PETITION: Most people focus in on the third purpose of prayer— asking the Almighty for something. "Lord, please let me pass this test, make the team, win this game, buy this house, etc., etc." If they really get desperate, most people start initiating bargains, like "Lord, if only you grant my request, I will go to church more, pray more, be a better person, etc., etc." As a social studies teacher, I know that in our country's early history, our government had a habit of making treaties with Native Americans that our leaders in Washington would routinely break when it was convenient for them to do so. Well, no government has broken contracts with its constituents more often than human beings have broken pledges with their God.

That having been said, people resort most often to the form of petition in their prayer life for several simple reasons: people are needy, prayer requests are effective, and the Lord Himself asks that we call upon him for favors. I want our son and daughter-in-law to come to me if they are in trouble because, out of love, I would not want them to anguish over a situation in which I could in any way be of assistance. How much more so is the God of Love concerned for his children and willing to help them if they only call upon his name (John 16:23-24, Luke 11:2, Matt. 7:7, Matt. 21:22)?

My wife, Patrice, had surgery in the summer of 2004 to remove her cancerous right kidney. Immediately prior to the operation, our daughter-in-law, Ellen, asked the surgeon, Dr. George Coseriu, if he would join us in a moment of prayer. Ellen held Patrice's hand and the doctor's hand while I held Patrice's other hand from the opposite side of the bed. We all bowed our heads as Ellen was inspired to say a beautiful prayer asking God to guide the hands of Dr. Coseriu during the operation, and thanking him for giving Patrice the spirit to face the operation with dignity and courage. In her prayer, Ellen said that Patrice was an example for so many others who were now supporting her with their thoughts and prayers. She concluded by saying how much we love our God who has guided us in the detection and elimination of this disease. After her prayer, Dr. George crossed himself and said that although he thought he had been prepared for surgery before, he was now more than ever ready to begin what he was confident would be a successful surgery. Ellen had taken the opportunity to direct all of us— patient, surgeon, and family—to a very positive, hopeful focus in this most difficult, stressful time in our lives.

Dr. Jerome Michelangelo, in his book, *The Anatomy of Hope: How People Prevail in the Face of Illness,* relates the effectiveness of what Ellen had just done in biological terms: "I found that there is an authentic biology of hope. Belief and expectation—the key elements of hope—can block pain by releasing the brain's endorphins. During the course of an illness, hope can be imagined as a domino effect, a chain reaction in which each link makes improvement more likely." Many more people would say that the spiritual effects of prayer defy a biological explanation. They would contend that prayer is effective for the patient, even if that person was in a coma and was just being supported by the prayers of others. These people would not try to explain the efficacy of prayer other than in terms of faith. Barbara Cawthorne Crafton, in her book, *Some Things You Just Have to Live With: Musings on Middle Age,* comments, "I have much less faith in human logic than I did when I was young. And more faith in God. I am much less sure about most things than I used to be. But I feel the pull of the love of God all the time and I don't care nearly as much about not understanding."

I think that many of us have episodes in our life where we have asked for and have felt the power of God's assistance, but are then reluctant or embarrassed to credit the resolution of our crisis to God's intervention. Near the end of my senior in high school, my sister Jean, who was twenty-two years old, died suddenly. I really had very little opportunity or desire to study for my final exams that I had to take immediately upon my return to school. The most difficult of my exams was my Latin test, which would involve translations taken from five of fifty selections; fifty vocabulary words from a possible five hundred; plus sections requiring the conjugation of verbs and the declension of nouns, pronouns, and adjectives. I decided that since I had an extremely limited time in which to study, I would make up my own test and focus on knowing that test very well. Then I prayed to my sister to help me in the task at hand.

When the test was handed out, I turned it over to see that my test was not merely close to the test that was handed out—it was the identical exam! As soon as I realized that, I put my head down on my test so that my classmates would not see my tears that were quickly flowing from my eyes. Fortunately, by the time the priest who was administering the exam came to ask me if I was OK, I had composed myself and told him, "Father, no problem. I just want to tell you in advance that I am going to ace this exam." I went on to register the highest score in the class and my highest test score of the year.

Before now, I have not often told this story because, frankly, I was embarrassed that either people would not believe me or they would think that I was crazy—that the chances of my making up the same exam as my professor are astronomically higher than picking the weekly lottery numbers. Or they might have thought that in my emotional state, I got the facts a little confused. But that event is indelibly imprinted on my mind and I will forever know that my sister interceded for me. And I believe that many people who have picked up this book on prayer either have similar stories or simply by faith believe my story to be true. For those who don't believe it, no measure of explanation will suffice.

SATISFACTION FOR SINS: The third neglected form of prayer is satisfaction for one's sins. One of our celebrities from whom we have solicited a prayer is Susan Luchsinger, Christian Country Music Association Female Vocalist of the Year for 1994 and 1995. Susan chose as her favorite prayer a psalm from King David: *"Search my heart, oh God; see if there be any wicked way within me."* Indeed, recognition is the first step in the process of forgiveness. No matter if you are a plumber, preacher, politician, or a pitcher, improvement comes only after admission of the need for improvement.

If one spouse has been hurtful toward his or her partner, the wound will not heal fully unless the offender makes amends for the transgression. The Amish have taken this practice to the max with their practice of "shunning." If an Old Order Amish breaks a religious prohibition, that person is to be avoided or shunned until the perpetrator has confessed the sin and asked forgiveness before the entire congregation. Most of us would view that punishment to be quite harsh, especially in our "me first" society that focuses on immediate gratification. However, we might be able to take some lessons from the Amish, whose emphasis on admission of sin and the need for forgiveness could possibly shore up many families in our general society.

If a child is disrespectful to his or her father, it would be appropriate that an immediate, though loving, correction is made. And so too, if we have turned our back on our Heavenly Father, shouldn't we also make "Amens" for our offenses?

Martin Luther, before he started the Lutheran religion, was a Catholic monk. He criticized the way the Catholic religion at the time had allowed people to make reparations for their sins. By donating some money or some land, a person would be granted an "indulgence," which would quicken the time by which a person could enter heaven. When I was a young boy, there were still remnants of this practice in the Catholic religion. I remember going on a yearly retreat in my middle-school years. During these retreats, we were always given some individual prayer time. I remember trying to find the shortest prayer with the longest indulgence, and then, as quickly as possible, reciting this prayer as many times as was possible in our allotted time. My prayer was always, "Jesus, Mary, and Joseph—I give you my heart and my soul." This short prayer would grant, if I remember correctly, several hundred years of indulgence. My friends and I decided we could shorten this prayer to "Jesus, Mary, and Joseph," and still gain the full indulgence. Then we took the liberty of further streamlining the prayer to "JMJ." If God were indeed all-knowing, he would have no problem recognizing the abbreviation "JMJ!" We felt rather proud of ourselves because we always gained for ourselves thousands and thousands of years of indulgence to cover a host of future transgressions. Obviously, our concept of prayer and the purpose of prayer was rather naïve.

Admitting that we are sinners and saying that we are sorry for our sins are indeed two very important aspects of prayer. Ultimately, we find it quite easy to accept God's forgiveness – quite another thing to extend forgiveness to others. For me, the most difficult aspect of my faith is forgiving someone who has wronged me or my family in some way. If someone has hurt me or, more importantly, has hurt someone I love, I find it extremely difficult to erase that experience from my mind. Feel sorry for the offender? Yes. Pray for him? Yes. Forgive him? Difficult, but doable. The Lord helps me with this one when He promises me in His most famous prayer that He will forgive me as I forgive others. Still, it's hard for me to again put myself in a situational relationship with that same person because I always feel that I will be taken advantage of – that I will be hurt again and have to forgive again. Lord, "seventy times seven (Matthew 18:22)" is a lot of forgiveness! I find it easier to just avoid some people and circumstances so as to preclude me and my family from being offended. I try to be aware of my failings in this regard. I pray for anyone whom I feel has wronged me and try to avoid confrontations as much as possible. And I rely on the Lord to continue to help me improve in this matter.

OK, we've talked about the purposes of prayer. But when is the best time to pray? St. Paul would encourage us to "pray without ceasing"(1 Thessalonians 5:17). Most people would say that in our fast-paced society, they don't have a single moment to spare. If they had more time, they would exercise, read a book, take a vacation, do home repairs, or any number of things that they continually put off because….well, they don't have the time. I feel that Martin Luther put this issue in perspective when he stated, "I have so much to do that I shall spend my first three hours in prayer."

I guess it's a matter of priorities: Some people can't find one hour in the 168-hour week to give praise and thanks to our God. Some people, on the other hand, find it essential that they start the day by attending daily mass so that they can organize their priorities and focus on what is important. An old fisherman once told me that the best time to fish is "when you have the time." And I think that most fishermen are going to prioritize their schedules so that there will always be some time to drop in a line. In much the same way, people who want to improve their prayer life have to find the time to "drop a line" to God their Father.

Some people with type-A personalities will say they don't have the time, not even to fish or do anything else except the essential things like working, preparing meals, maintaining the house, and taking care of the kids. Then I would suggest that they layer in prayer on top of things they already do. You eat, so for ten seconds, give thanks before the meal. You wash the dishes? You make the bed? You take out the garbage? You stop at a stoplight? Program yourself to say even a little prayer (How about "Jesus, Mary, and Joseph, I give you my heart and my soul?") at these times. A person's lifestyle might determine when it is most convenient for him or her to pray. During the last twelve years of my teaching career, I drove twenty-two miles to my high school. I made it a practice to say the rosary at the beginning of each morning transit. I must confess that I did not know all the names or the proper sequence of the glorious, sorrowful, or joyful mysteries that are attached to each decade of the rosary. I resigned myself to saying what I called the "generic" rosary without any designation for any specific decade. In preparing this book, I found out that former Notre Dame coach, Gerry Faust, also finds it convenient, easy, and soothing to pray a rosary or several rosaries while he's driving to an appointment.

I think that most people would improve their prayer life if they only thought of a couple of simple concepts. First of all, our life on earth is infinitesimally short when compared to our existence in the next life. If you calculate the average age of people you see in churches, you will see that it takes quite a few years for most people to figure this out—but eventually, a lot do. In his song, "Live Like You Were Dying," Tim McGraw feels that people's lives would be enriched by the acceptance of the certainty of their ultimate passing from this life.

Secondly, most parents want to keep a steady communication with their children when their kids grow up and live on their own.

Simply put, if parents don't hear from their brood for a length of time, they themselves start to "brood." Most of us can relate to those feelings of longing, anxiety, frustration, and disappointment if contact is cut off from our children for even a brief period of time. Why is it so easy, then, to be insensitive to our failure to communicate with our Heavenly Father?

Once we recognize the necessity of prayer and reflect upon the opportunities for prayer, the question most often asked is "How do we pray?" One of the major purposes of this book is to help people answer this question. I have selected a great number of celebrities to share with us their favorite prayer. Why celebrities? Why do companies pay celebrities outrageous amounts of money to model shoes or soft drinks? Because whether it is deserved or not, these people have the attention of the public. It seemed to me that if celebrities can convince us to consume a unique type of food choice, to buy a particular brand of car, or to wear a distinctive style of clothing, then why not use them to help persuade us how to pray? It's amazing to me what crazy fashions (tattoos and piercings) and extreme behavior our youth will adopt because they are modeled by some celebrities. This book hopefully will enable people of all ages to realize that in the practice of prayer, there is a more positive modeling that can be copied. I have made contact with some wonderful, terrific people while compiling this book. Many of these people don't think of themselves as anything special—but they are. To me, the people in this book are special not only for what they may have accomplished in society, but also for the fact that they were not afraid to admit that they pray; moreover, they were not afraid to share their method of prayer, and they were not afraid or embarrassed about what this admission might do to their public image as a star.

How did I come upon the idea for this book? During my teaching career, I started the practice of contacting celebrities and encouraging them to send a picture with some words of encouragement to my students. Each week, I would display a different celebrity's picture with their quotation. This teaching tool proved quite effective. I was surprised by how many stars sent their pictures. Moreover, I couldn't believe the creativity and effort a number of these famous people put into their reflections. Actor Tony Randall quoted Socrates, and basketball coach Denny Crum quoted Winston Churchill!

So, it was easy for me to transfer this technique to come up with the idea of asking these celebrities to participate in a much more important endeavor. I simply asked these same people (and many, many more) to share with me their favorite prayer for inclusion in a book.

I was excited as I sent out the first batch of several hundred letters. However, my task this time would prove to be much more difficult. First of all, finding current and valid addresses for celebrities who understandably value their privacy is a very difficult task. It takes hours and hours of research and determination. Secondly, even when an address is found, the tragedy of 9/11 has made famous people more reluctant to personally open their own mail or to accept fan mail at all. Most major celebrities today have agents and secretaries to handle their mail. These "gatekeepers" are hired to protect the privacy of their clients while providing some access to the public. The easiest way to do this is by sending out a picture with either a stamped or personalized signature.

I am not in any way condemning the celebrities who did not participate. I myself am very selective in regard to the mail I respond to, and I don't have the packed schedule that these celebrities do. I am just relating the difficulties I encountered, for several reasons. Reaching celebrities and getting responses more than an autograph is an extremely difficult process, and the people who did respond apparently were truly committed to the objective I had in mind.

Several celebrities (Father Joseph Girzone, Art Linkletter, Dom Dimaggio, and John McVay) related that they believe that prayer is simply an intimate, personalized conversation with God. Therefore, these people could not send a particular "favorite" prayer. I totally agree with their definition of prayer. I also agree with John McVay, who wrote that he realized the importance of formalized prayer to "'get us started' talking to God." This is a major purpose of this book. We could all probably agonize each holiday writing our own cards to our loved ones (and I would even encourage such efforts). However, American Greetings and Hallmark have made this process easier for us by producing cards that express the sentiments we feel. The celebrities in this book have provided us with beautiful reflections that hopefully will serve to lift our hearts and minds to God.

I pondered quite a while as to how I would catalog the celebrities and their prayers. I could have displayed them by careers or by similar types of prayer responses (e.g. Biblical passages, formalized prayer, personally created prayer, etc.). Ultimately, I decided to simply present the celebrities alphabetically. This method would aid the reader in more quickly locating the stars and their prayers. At the same time, I realize that this method produces some duplication of prayer responses. I decided that this may not be a bad thing. This small amount of repetition might underline for the reader the prayers that have had the highest efficacy and comfort level for our celebrity responders.

I might add that I have called these people "celebrities," not "saints." And some are of local fame, while the reputation of others is worldwide. I'm sure that some readers are bound to question the inclusion of one or more stars in this compilation. I urge the reader to leave the final judgment as to each celebrity's worth as a role model to the "Final Judge." I hope that readers open their minds to what the "stars" have to give them, not to what they can take away from the "stars."

One final personal note: It has taken me more than five years to put this book together. During this time, my wife has had five major operations. I only hope that the prayers that these wonderful celebrities have sent me have as much meaning for you and provide you with the same strength that they have provided my wife and me during our difficult times. As a result, I hope that your own personal prayer life will become enriched. I hope these prayers will be a comfort and inspiration to you as you continue on your journey back to God. May that journey become more focused and the trek a little smoother by your reading of this *Book of Prayers: To the Heavens from the Stars.*

Scotty Alexander – Musician

One of the best pluses of living in Ashville, New York, is our proximity to the Chautauqua Institution. This vibrant summer community provides an atmosphere of learning and culture for the whole family. The Institution was founded back in 1874 as a training center for Methodist Sunday school teachers. Over the years, it has blossomed into a nondenominational mecca for vacationers who are looking to both relax and to refresh their minds.

Every Friday night throughout a nine-week summer season, Chautauqua features popular entertainers who perform in Chautauqua's historic amphitheater.

Several years ago, my wife and I went to see Wayne Newton in concert at Chautauqua. I was most impressed with the quality of Wayne's band and his backup singers. One musician in particular stood out in regard to his versatility and the quality of his performance. He was so good that my wife and I both made it a point to seek him out after the concert in order to commend him on his showmanship. That man, Scotty Alexander, is Wayne Newton's musical director.

It turns out that Scotty was a child prodigy who recorded his first record, *Here I Come World*, at the age of six! He quickly mastered the guitar, fiddle, mandolin, five-string bass, banjo, drums, and piano. At the age of thirteen, he appeared on *Star Search*.

Throughout Alexander's young career, he has been privileged to have opened for Bob Hope and Mel Tillis and to play for a wide variety of TV commercials and movie soundtracks. Scotty has toured as part of many bands of popular performers, and he has participated in a number of USO overseas shows for the troops.

Scotty is married, and he and his wife Lisa have three children. My wife and I were impressed by his talent on the stage and his winning personality as he talked with us after the concert.

At the concert Scotty said that he'd be glad to send a prayer for my project, and true to his word, this is the beautiful, personal prayer that he sent:

> *"Dear God, I pray to you in the name of your SON, JESUS CHRIST. When all of this is over and I look back on the life you blessed me with, please let my greatest earthly accomplishments be the love and relationships I shared with my wife Lisa and our three kids. Please help me be the father and husband that you would want so that Tanna, Tarryn, and Niiko have a solid foundation for this life.*
>
> *I pray for the parents of all the kids fighting the war and those in hospitals tonight watching over a sick child. Please let this prayer give them and their children strength and hope. Please watch over my own children.*
>
> *Thank you for all my blessings. I want to do the best I can with the talents you have given me so that I can fill the spirits of all those around me.*

And please Dear GOD, when my work is done, can I play and sing for you?

In JESUS' name, I pray. AMEN!!

Kim Alexis – Model

When I was teaching U.S. History in Cleveland, Ohio, I took a busload of students each year to New York to visit Fort Niagara. While we were there we also visited the Niagara Power Plant and then ate lunch at a McDonalds that had formerly been an historic hotel on a stagecoach route. Fort Niagara is an awesome fort strategically located where the Niagara River enters Lake Ontario. Historically, whoever controlled that fort controlled the pathway to the interior of the northwestern frontier. I think that the students were most impressed by the beauty of the location.

I didn't know until writing this book that the area is also associated with another item of beauty. The nearby town of Lockport is the birthplace of model Kim Alexis. Kim has appeared on more than 500 magazine covers and her image has been displayed in six of Sports Illustrated Swim Suit editions.

Kim was born and raised in Lockport and, while in high school, excelled on the swim team and also participated in the band. After high school she had intended to pursue a pharmaceutical career; however, she went into modeling first, originally with the intention of raising money for college.

In reading Kim's bio, I discovered that she has an inner as well as outer beauty. The life of a supermodel would seem to most to be a life of complete ease. However, the pressures of extreme dietary demands put a lot of stress on her body and her self esteem. She also suffered through a divorce. Then, in 1990, Kim gave herself over to Jesus Christ.

She is now married to NHL star Ron Duguay. Kim and Ron have a blended family and Kim loves her busy and fulfilling life raising the three boys and two girls.

Kim has written a book entitled *A Model for a Better Future.* I haven't read the book yet; but the title seems to sum up the way this beautiful lady has triumphed over her earlier challenges.

(Not many people know that this model has run, at last count, eight marathons!)

Kim sent us her favorite biblical passage which is taken from Philippians 4: 4-9:

> *Rejoice in the Lord always. I will say it again: Rejoice! Let your gentleness be evident to all. The Lord is near. Do not be anxious about anything, but in everything, by prayer and petition, with thanksgiving, present your requests to God. And the peace of God, which transcends all understanding, will guard your hearts and minds in Christ Jesus.*
>
> *Finally, brothers, whatever is true, whatever is noble, whatever is right, whatever is pure, whatever is lovely, whatever is admirable – if anything is excellent or*

praiseworthy — think about such things. Whatever you have learned or received or heard from me, or seen in me — put into practice. And the God of peace will be with you.

Steve Alford –
Basketball player and coach

Steve Alford was respected as a player and now is respected as a coach. But, ultimately, I think that Steve would want to be remembered for the qualities he possesses as a husband, a father, and a friend.

Steve and his wife Tanya have been friends since their days as classmates back in elementary school. They were married in 1987 and now have three children.

Alford has had a stellar career in basketball both as a player and as a coach. He averaged 37.7 points per game as a high school senior playing for his father at New Castle Chrysler High School. He was named Indiana's "Mr. Basketball" as well as Converse High School National Player of the Year.

As a college freshman, he was selected as a member of the U.S. Olympic Basketball Team (along with other collegians Michael Jordan, Patrick Ewing, Sam Perkins, Chris Mullins, and Wayman Tisdale).

Steve earned first team All-Big Ten honors in each of his final three collegiate seasons. He earned recognition as MVP of the Big Ten his senior year. Alford captained the 1987 Indiana team that won the NCAA tournament championship. Steve graduated from Indiana University with a degree in business.

Steve played four years in the pros (with Dallas and Golden State), and he coached four years in Division III at Manchester College and four years at Southwest Missouri State. While at Manchester, he was named Indiana Collegiate Conference Coach of the Year for 1993, 1994, and 1995. Alfred was at the helm at Iowa from 2000 through 2007 before being named head coach at the University of New Mexico.

In response to my prayer request, Steve wrote that he felt that "prayers are personal and in my case ever changing." But he said that a verse that he frequently turns to in the Bible is from James, one of his favorite books of the Bible. The quote he refers to is from James 1:12:

> *"Blessed is anyone who endures temptation. Such a one has stood the test and will receive the crown of life that the Lord has promised to those who love him."*

June Allyson – Actress

What do the following people have in common: Marion Morrison, Allen Stewart Konigsberg, Vincent Furnier, Harold

Jenkins, Reginald Dwight, Joseph Levitch, Richard Sharkey, Anna Mae Bullock, and Ella Geisman? They all are better known by their famous stage names.

Ella Geisman is actually June Allyson, a well-known movie star of the 1940s and 1950s. She now is recognized by today's contemporary audience as the TV spokeswoman for Depends.

June was injured in a fall when she was eight years old and had to wear a steel brace the next four years. Her recovery was hastened by water therapy and eventually dance. It was her study of dance that led to her later stardom.

June was signed as the understudy to Betty Hutton (birth name: Elizabeth June Thornburg) in the musical *Panama Hattie*. Miss Allyson took over when Betty came down with the measles. Her performance impressed director George Abbott, who signed her as a lead in his next musical (1941) "Best Foot Forward." From Broadway, Allyson played the same role when the play was made into a movie (1943).

In 1945, June married actor Dick Powell. The couple had a son, Dick Powell Jr. June also adopted Dick's daughter, Pamela Powell. After Dick Powell died of cancer in 1963, June married Glen Maxwell. The couple divorced in 1970. June has been married to Dr. David Ashrow since 1976.

Allyson has been featured in some prominent classic films such as *3 Musketeers* (1948) and *Little Women* (1949). She also starred opposite some famous leading men. She shared the screen three times with Jimmy Stewart: *The Stratton Story* (1949), *The Glenn Miller Story* (1954), and *Strategic Air Command* (1955).

Miss Allyson's image is heightened in my mind since she shares a birthday with my wife, Patrice, on October 7.

Oh, by the way, I know you want to know the stage names of those other people listed above, so here they are:

Marion Morrison = John Wayne

Allen Stewart Konigsberg = Woody Allen

Vincent Furnier = Alice Cooper

Harold Jenkins = Conway Twitty

Reginald Dwight = Elton John

Joseph Levitch = Jerry Lewis

Richard Starkey = Ringo Starr

Anna Mae Bullock = Tina Turner

June Allyson sent this beautiful prayer:

> I said a prayer for you today
> And know God must have heard –
> I felt the answer in my heart
> Although He spoke no word.
> I didn't ask for wealth or fame,
> I knew you wouldn't mind,
> I asked Him to send treasures
> Of a far more lasting kind.
> I asked that He'd be near you
> At the start of each new day
> To grant you health and blessings
> And friends to share your way.
> I asked for happiness for you
> In all things great and small –
> But it was for His loving care,
> I prayed the most of all.

Leah O'Brien-Amico –
Three time Olympic gold medalist, softball

It always amazes me how accomplished so many of the celebrities are who have sent in prayer responses! Case in point—Leah O'Brien-Amico. By the age of thirty she had earned gold medals in three consecutive summer Olympic competitions (Atlanta, Georgia; Sydney, Australia; and Athens, Greece) as a member of the U.S. Women's Olympic softball team.

Leah helped lead the University of Arizona Wildcats to three Women's College World Series titles (1993, 1994, and 1997) while also meriting three Academic All-American honors.

Leah's career has had "winner" written all over it as the teams she has played on have won gold medals in the 1999 and 2003 Pan American Games as well as the 1998 and 2002 ISF World Championships. Somehow during this time, she managed to play with the California Commotion, a team that won the ASA National Championship in 1999.

Leah O'Brien married Tommy Amico in January of 1999 and the couple now have a son, Jake.

Leah sent me "A Prayer of Salvation." She further explained that "The Bible teaches that if you confess with your mouth, 'Jesus is Lord,' and believe in your heart that God raised him from the dead, you will be saved" (Romans 10:9).

<u>A Prayer of Salvation</u>

Lord Jesus,

I realize I need you and want you in my life. I want to make you the Lord and Savior of my life. Jesus, I thank you for dying on the cross for my sins and the sins of the whole world. Thank you for forgiving my sins I have committed against you and for giving me eternal life with you. Please guide me and direct me and allow your will to be done in my life. Change me from the inside out and make me the person you want me to be. Amen.

Patty Berg – Legendary women's golf champion

A natural athlete as a youth, Patty's parents steered her into golf to distract her from her prowess on the neighborhood football team.

Patty became a professional at the age of twenty-two and won an endorsement from Wilson Sporting Goods. Patty earned her early money by giving clinics and exhibitions.

After an eighteen-month layoff due to a severe automobile accident in 1941, Patty won several championships and then entered the Marines during World War II.

After the war, she was the founder and first president of the Ladies Professional Golf Association in 1948. Patty won thirty-nine LPGA tournaments over the next eleven years.

The Associated Press named Patty Woman Athlete of the Year in three different decades (1938, 1943, and 1955). The LPGA now annually gives the Patty Berg Award for outstanding contributions to women's golf.

Patty Berg wrote that her favorite prayer, "now and throughout my life, is and always has been the Lord's Prayer. I recite it at least once a day, and at critical times in my life have turned to it for both inner strength and reassurance. It truly was and is a guidepost in my life."

The Our Father (Matthew 6:9-13 & Luke 11: 2-4)*
9v. Our Father, who art in Heaven,
Hallowed be thy name.
10 v. Thy kingdom come, thy will be done,
On earth as it is in Heaven.
11v. Give us this day our daily bread
12v. And forgive us our tresspasses
13v. As we forgive those who trespass against us.
And lead us not into temptation,
But deliver us from evil.

For thine is the kingdom, and the power, and the glory, for ever.
Amen.

Yogi Berra –
Great New York Yankee Catcher

If you are a baseball fan, you've probably, at one time or another, had a discussion based on "What is the best 'Yogi-ism'?" And I'm sure that the candidates would include:

It ain't over until it's over.
It's déjà vu all over again.
When you come to the fork in the road – take it.
I didn't really say everything I said.
It gets late early out here.
If the people don't want to come to the ballpark,
nobody's going to stop them.
You can observe a lot by watching.

These malapropisms almost overshadow the fact that Lawrence P. "Yogi" Berra was one of the greatest catchers of all time. Yogi (a nickname given by a childhood friend who thought he resembled a yogi, i.e., a practitioner of the Hindu exercise of yoga).

Before he made the major leagues, Yogi joined the Navy during World War II. Few people know that Berra participated in the D-Day invasion off Omaha Beach.

Yogi was called up to the big leagues shortly after the war. In a sign of what was to come, Berra hit a home run in his very first game. It was one of 380 home runs he would hit in his 19 year career with the Yankees.

In his career Berra was named to the All-star team 15 times. He's a member of the All Century team and ultimately, in 1972, he was inducted into baseball's Hall of Fame.

Yogi was a member of 10 World Championship teams (more than any other player in history). He led great Yankee teams in RBI's for seven straight seasons (1945-1955). He caught two no hitters, one by Allie Reynolds in 1951 and the other, the only perfect game in World Series history, by Don Larsen in 1956. The picture of Yogi jumping into Larsen's arms is one of the most recognizable photographs in baseball history. He once played 148 straight games without making an error in 950 chances.

Yogi hit the third most home runs (12) in World Series history, bested only by Micky Mantle (18) and Babe Ruth (15).

After his playing days, Yogi managed both the Yankees (1964) and the Mets (1973) to pennants in their respective leagues.

As you read through these celebrity introductions, I think you will find that marital longevity is a characteristic shared by many of the participants. Yogi and his wife, Carmen, have been married over 50 years and have three sons and ten grandchildren.

Yogi is justifiably proud of the Yogi Berra Museum and Learning Center.

Well, my introduction's not over 'til it's over – and it's over – but, there are still lot's of more introductions to come.

Yogi's prayer:

> *"Dear Lord, I thank you for all your blessings throughout my life. I ask you to bless my family day after day.*

And remember all of my friends and relatives who lost their loved ones."

Bobby Bowden – FSU football coach

When I was working on my master's degree at West Virginia University in the early 1970s, Morgantown was a very small, rural location. Its basketball coliseum had just opened, construction had just started on the People Mover, and the football team was still playing in the old stadium in the middle of the downtown campus.

There was no cable TV at the time, and the only three shows that we liked that came in clearly each week were Marlin Perkins's *Wild Kingdom, McMillan and Wife,* and *Coach Bobby Bowden's Football Show.* My wife— who is not a sports fan—would never miss Coach Bowden's show. Not only was Bobby knowledgeable, but he had a wholesome, down-home humor that was endearing to his many fans.

Coach Bowden had been a Little All American quarterback from Howard College (now Samford University) in 1953. He was named head coach of the Mountaineers in 1970 and compiled a 42-26 record in his six years at the school. He then went to Florida State in 1976 where he was 5-6-0 in his first year. He has not had a losing season since, and in 1993, his Seminoles were national champions. As this book is being published, Bowden and Coach Joe Paterno have been coaching the same number of years and are the top two coaches in regard to their number of victories at the major college level. The two are also the only Division I coaches to have won twenty or more bowl games.

In 2004, the Fellowship of Christian Athletes established the National Bobby Bowden Award, given annually to one football player in the country for his achievements on the field, in the classroom, and in the community.

Bobby and his wife Ann have six children.

(Note: In 1943, when Bobby was thirteen years old, he was diagnosed with rheumatic fever. After six months in the hospital, Bowden spent over a year confined to bed fighting this illness. My brother-in-law, Marty Lydecker, who is a band director and sports fan, will be glad to know that because of his condition, young Bobby Bowden became quite the trombone player in the band and orchestra before he was given the OK to once again play football.)

Coach Bowden sent a prayer that "I have made with my coaches and players before every ball game. Our prayer may vary some each game, but not much."

Dear God,

Thank you for letting us play football. Thank you for the strong, healthy bodies you have given us to compete. We do not come to you today to pray for victory but to ask for your guidance. We pray that you will protect us from injury as well as our opponents. We ask you to heal our players who will miss today's game today with an injury. Also, we pray that you will help us do our best...after all, that is all we can do...our best!

I pray that you will give our Coaches wisdom in decisions we must make. I pray that we all be positive examples for all the young people that are watching us. Most of all, whatever the outcome, we pray that we can glorify you.

We ask this in Christ's Name, Amen.

Dan Britton –
Senior VP of ministries for FCA

Dan Britton is the senior vice president of ministries for the Fellowship of Christian Athletes (FCA). Dan was quite an athlete himself. In high school, he won all-conference and state recognition in both football and lacrosse.

At the University of Delaware, while earning his finance degree, he captained his lacrosse team and then was drafted by the Baltimore Thunder in the Professional Indoor Lacrosse League. Dan was an all-star and four-year starter with the Thunder.

After his professional career, Britton joined with the FCA. In his current position, he has a wide range of responsibilities that include camps, coaches' ministry, and campus ministry. Each year,

FCA programs reach more than a million people. FCA campus units are called "huddles," and there are "huddles" on 8,000 campuses where student athletes meet for prayer, fellowship, and Bible study.

Dan is now serving at the FCA headquarters in Kansas City. He and his wife Dawn have three children.

Dan included as his favorite reflection the Fellowship of Christian Athletes Prayer for Athletes and Coaches:

Dear Father –

I am realizing that we need You in America more than ever before. There's so much pain and hurt and, God, I know that You are the only One who can heal our Land. Now, more than ever, God, I'm aware of how crucial it is to live out Your love, Your grace, and Your power. As athletes walk the halls of their schools, and compete on the fields and courts, I pray that they have a passionate commitment to serve others with –

> *Tender hearts beating with integrity,*
> *Focused eyes vividly seeing what can be,*
> *Listening ears hearing wise counsel,*
> *Teachable souls surrendering to the Holy Spirit,*
> *Tame tongues speaking truth and righteousness,*
> *Pierced hearts experiencing Your love,*
> *Serving hands washing the feet of others,*
> *Loud voices proclaiming Your Truth,*
> *Clean feet walking a pure life.*

God, I stand in the gap for all athletes and coaches. I cry out and lift my voice in prayer for them. You have prepared me for such a time as this. Thank you for the ministry of FCA. Thank you for using the FCA staff, athletes, coaches, and the student leaders to powerfully impact their campuses for Christ. Youth need you so desperately. It's time to do battle for the souls of our youth, God—let's see You take the schools by storm! Amen.

John Brockington –
Fullback: Ohio State and Green Bay

1971 was a very good collegiate draft year for the National Football League. The players from that year who are familiar to most sports fans include John Riggins, Lyle Alzado, Jim Plunkett, Archie Manning, Dan Postorini, JD Hill, Jack Tatum, Jack Youngblood, Dan Dierdorf, Phil Villapiano, Jim Braxton (WVU grad and blocking back for O.J. Simpson), Ken Anderson, Joe Theismann, Mel Gray, and Harold Carmichael. Also in that draft are three football players who are also included in this book: Doug Dieken (who wrote the Foreword) and Ohio State players Rex Kern and John Brockington.

Rex Kern was the quarterback and John Brockington was the fullback for the Buckeye teams that from 1968 to 1970 went

27-2, and won three Big Ten Championships and two National Championships. In 1970, Brockington rushed for 1,142 yards and 17 touchdowns. OSU's chance for an undefeated season that year was ruined only by the team's 27-17 defeat in the Rose Bowl by Jim Plunkett's Stanford Cardinal team.

John was a first-round pick (ninth overall) of the Green Bay Packers. He was the NFL's Rookie of the Year in 1971, when he ran for a then-rookie record of 1,105 yards. He became the first player in NFL history to rush for 1,000 yards in each of his first three seasons. And it only took John four seasons to become the second leading rusher in Packer history.

However, John's numbers started to fade and his career was over after only six years.

Now, fast forward over five years to find John forming a friendship with Packer fan Diane Cogan, a literary professor at the University of California at San Diego. A few years later, in 2000, John became ill and his potassium levels were dangerously low. He was put on dialysis until a kidney donor could be found. Tests revealed that Diane was a perfect match, and in 2001, she donated her kidney to her friend. John and Diane ultimately decided that they indeed were a match and these two friends became husband and wife on August 16, 2003.

Diane was kind enough to email me John's favorite biblical passage from Isaiah 41:10:

> *"Do not fear, for I am with you, do not be afraid, for*
> *I am your God; I will strengthen you, I will help you,*
> *I will uphold you with my victorious right hand."*

Lane Brody –
Singer/songwriter/actress

Country singer/songwriter/actress Lane Brody's birth name was actually Eleni (Greek for Lane) Connie Voorhas.

In her youth, Lane was a talented gymnast, specializing in the balance beam. She dreamed about one day being an Olympian. As it turned out, Lane would indeed ultimately be involved in the 1984 Los Angeles Olympics. However, her association would be as a singer for the catchy Beatrice Foods commercial, "You've Known Us All Along" which was played throughout the televised Olympics.

Lane is famous for recording the following songs: "You're Gonna Make Love to Me," "Over You" (Oscar-nominated song), "The Yellow Rose" (she reworked this Civil War standard into a number-one hit on the country music charts), "All the Unsung Heroes" (honoring Vietnam veterans), "He Burns Me Up," "He's Taken," and "Baby's Eyes."

The multitalented Miss Brody has sung jingles, modeled, and appeared in a number of TV episodes. She has a special love for animals and each year sponsors a benefit for "Walden's Puddle," a nonprofit organization devoted to the care of sick and injured native Tennessee wildlife. I think it's appropriate for this book to note that Lane has adopted an abandoned starling bird. She named the bird Fevronia Starling and, among other phrases, she has taught it to say, "Glory to God."

☆ ☆ ☆

Lane gave this response to our prayer request:

> *"As an Orthodox Christian I do my best to pray unceasingly*
> *— I pray for Our Father to bless and protect all His creation*
> *and all the sick, suffering captives (human and animal)*
> *for their salvation and always Lord Jesus Christ Son of*
> *God Have mercy on me a sinner (known as the prayer of*
> *the Heart). God bless you."*

Betty Buckley – Broadway star

Of course, a cultural illiterate like myself will always associate Betty Buckley with the four years she portrayed Sandra Sue "Abby" Abbot Bradford on TV's *Eight Is Enough*. Actually, when Betty played the part of Abby, she was actually in real life younger than Laurie Walters, who played Joannie Bradford, the second oldest of the Bradford daughters. See, I told you that I am more focused on Betty's *Eight Is Enough* role rather than her sizeable reputation as a legend in musical theater.

Betty Lynn Buckley got her first taste of the theater when she was eleven years old and her mother took her to see a production of *The Pajama Game,* which was choreographed by Bob Fosse. Eventually, in 1973, Buckley would portray Catherine in the musical *Pippin,* choreographed by her early idol, Bob Fosse.

Betty attended Texas Christian University, was named Miss Fort Worth, and in 1966, was runner-up in the Miss Texas pageant. Her talent was so outstanding that she was asked to perform for the 1967 Miss America Pageant as well as to travel to Korea and Japan for troops that had been wounded during the Vietnam War.

At the young age of twenty-two, Betty landed the part of Martha Jefferson in the original version of the musical *1776.* In the Broadway production of *Carrie,* Buckley played Carrie's mother, Margaret White. Interestingly, in the film version of *Carrie,* Betty was cast to play the gym teacher.

One of Betty's most heralded performances would be her Tony award-winning role as Grizabella the Glamour Cat in Andrew Lloyd Webber's *Cats.*

Buckley has quite a remarkable and versatile resume of theater engagements, record albums, and TV and film credits; but I am still reminiscing about *Eight Is Enough.* After all, Brian Patrick Clarke—who played Merle "The Pearl" Stockwell on the series—graduated from Shaker Heights High School in Ohio, albeit some years before I taught there.

Ms. Buckley's favorite prayer is the prayer of St. Francis:

Lord make me an instrument of your peace.
Where there is hatred, let me sow love,
where there is injury, pardon,
where there is doubt, faith,
where there is despair, hope,

where there is darkness, light,
and where there is sadness, joy.

Grant that I may not so much seek
to be consoled as to console,
to be understood, as to understand,
to be loved as to love,
for it is in giving that we receive,
it is in pardoning that we are pardoned,
and it is in dying, that we are born to eternal life.

Dyan Cannon – Movie/TV Actress

Dyan Cannon was born Samile Diane Friesen. Dyan defies the effects of age on her person and on her professional success. She is a beauty today even as she was a beauty when she won the title of Miss West Seattle back in 1955.

In earlier times, she was best known for her 1965 marriage to superstar Cary Grant, who was thirty-three years her senior. Cannon and Grant had one child, Jennifer, who is also in the entertainment business and appeared in the TV show *Beverly Hills 90210*.

She emerged as a star in her own right with her breakout movie, *Bob and Carol and Ted and Alice* (she was "Alice" and Natalie Wood was "Carol").

Cannon and Grant were divorced in 1968. At some point after the divorce, Dyan found religion and became outspoken about her Christian beliefs. Cannon tried marriage again in 1984 when she wed Stanley Fimberg. That union, too, ended in divorce, in 1990.

In recent years, Dyan has been best known as a regular on *Ally McBeal* and *Three Sisters*.

Dyan Cannon can be seen quite often cheering on her beloved Los Angeles Lakers at the Staples Center.

In 2001, Dyan escaped harm after a fire that started in her kitchen spread throughout her condominium.

☆　　☆　　☆

Dyan Cannon sends this prayer which is short, sweet, and to the point:

> *"Dear God, thank you for loving me and everyone so we can always feel loved. Amen."*

Kristen Chenoweth – Actress/singer

Kristen Chenoweth is one very talented and busy lady. Most importantly, her life seems to embody perfectly the theme that I have adopted for this book. In an interview with Debra Akins for

Today's Christian magazine (Sept/Oct 2005), Kristen stated: "I've always wanted to let people know that there are real people in the real world trying to be what God wants them to be."

Kristen, who is adopted, seemed to always value her religion as she also developed her musical talents. At an early age she desired to become a missionary. She earned her master's degree in voice from Oklahoma City University and was runner-up for the 1991 title of Miss Oklahoma. A full scholarship would have allowed her to continue her training at the Philadelphia Academy of Vocal Arts. However, two weeks before school was to start she won a theater audition in New York City and her path in the entertainment industry - especially musical theater - was secured.

The multitalented Chenoweth has appeared on TV as Kristen Yancey in her own sitcom, *Kristin* (2001), as Portia on an episode of *Frasier* (2001), as Miss Noodle on *Sesame Street* (2003), as Marian Paroo on *The Music Man* (2003), as Annabeth Schott on *West Wing* (2004-2006), and as Olive Snook in *Pushing Daisies* (2007).

Kristin earned a Tony award for her performance as five-year-old Sally in the Broadway production of *You're a Good Man, Charlie Brown* (1998-1999) and a Tony nomination for playing Glinda, the Good Witch, in the play *Wicked* (2003).

Kristen has produced several albums including *Let Yourself Go* (2002), a collection of old standards, and *As I Am* (2005), a compilation of her favorite spirituals.

Ms. Chenoweth has somehow also found time to appear on the big screen in productions that have included *Bewitched, The Pink Panther, RV,* and *Deck the Halls*.

Kristen sent a handwritten copy of her favorite prayer, a slightly abridged version of The Prayer of St. Francis:

Lord, make me an instrument of thy peace.
Where there is hatred, let me sow love.
Where there is darkness, let there be light.
Where there is sadness, let me sow joy.
Oh, Divine Master! Grant that I may not so much seek
To be consoled, as to console.

Tara Dawn Holland Christensen – Miss America 1997

The history of the Miss America program is a fascinating one. This beauty/talent competition began in Atlantic City, New Jersey in 1921 with the crowning of 16 year old Margaret Gorman who represented Washington, D.C. Incidentally, Miss Gorman was only 5'1" tall with measurements of 30-25-32 – a far cry from the statuesque beauties of today!

Today the Miss America pageant provides the largest source of educational scholarships available for young women in America. While other beauty competitions seem to look strictly for models, the Miss America organization searches for beautiful women who are also role models.

Few people know about another spin off pageant held for the first runners-up from each Miss America state pageant. This competition, not officially tied into the Miss America program, is held annually in Hoopeston, Illinois and culminates in the crowning of Miss National Sweetheart. Five of the past winners of this crown actually have reentered the state competitions and have gone on to win the title of Miss America*. The most recent pageant winner to have followed this path is Miss National Sweetheart of 1995, Tara Dawn Holland who in 1997 was crowned Miss America.

After her reign, Tara graduated with highest honors with a master's degree in music education from the University of Missouri-Kansas City in 2002.

Tara's goal of pursuing the title of Miss America began back in the 7th grade when she attended a concert given by Cheryl Prewitt, Miss America 1980.

Her platform while competing in the national pageant centered around literacy education. Tara is now in demand not only as a singer but as a speaker/advocate dedicated to encouraging youth to abstain from drugs, alcohol, and premarital sex.

Tara married Jon Christensen in 1998. They have one child, Petra Dawn.

If you have ever seen the movie, *Little Miss Sunshine*, there is a clip at the very beginning of the film showing Tara receiving her crown as Miss America.

*I know you'd want to know the five Miss Americas who first won the title of Miss National Sweetheart. They are: Elizabeth Ward (MA 1982), Debbye Turner (MA 1990), Carolyn Sapp (MA 1992), Leanza Cornett (MA 1993), and Tara Holland (MA 1997).

Just as I acknowledged Mary Lou Retton for being the very first celebrity to send in a prayer for this book, I am so grateful that I was able to include the very last one that came just under the wire from Tara Holland Christensen. I can't believe how beautifully instructive her prayer is for all of us! With Tara's gorgeous prayer I finish this book two days before Thanksgiving. I couldn't have asked for a better prayer to finish off the book! Here are Tara's comments and the prayer that she sent:

For me, there is not a favorite prayer that I repeat to the Lord. However, I do follow a specific outline almost every day as I talk to Him. It is an acronym based on the Lord's Prayer that reminds me of how to approach God. The acronym is ACTS:

Adoration — praising God for WHO He is, not just His miracles, provisions, and blessings. I find that this helps me to place God on His rightful throne in my mind.

Confession — admitting I am a sinner in need of the forgiveness only He can provide. Now, God is in the right place (through Adoration), and so am I, as I humbly present myself and my sins to Him.

Thanksgiving — thanking Him for the many blessings and provisions He has so faithfully given. I enjoy listing my blessings, such as air conditioning, clothes, friends, etc.

Supplication — presenting my requests to God, for myself and others.

I know God loves to hear His Word repeated back to Him, so whenever possible, I include His promises in my prayers.

I usually conclude with a reminder to myself and God that ultimately, I want only what God wants. As Jesus prayed, "Not my will, but Yours be done."

Here is an example of a prayer I might lift up:

Heavenly Father,

I praise and honor You, for You alone are worthy of worship. You are perfect in all Your ways. You are Holy, righteous, and just. You are my Redeemer, my Healer, my Refuge, and my Strong Tower. God, You are my Provider and the only God of peace. You are "I Am," and I praise You.

I confess to You that I am a sinner, asking Your forgiveness. I repent of my disobedience to You and the many times that You have spoken to me, but I was too occupied to even listen. Thank You for sending Your only Son, Jesus, to the cross to die for all my sins. Cleanse me, Lord, and make me whole. Thank you for restoring me.

Thank you for the tremendous blessings in my life -- my incredible, Godly husband, our wonderful daughter, and my precious parents. I give you all thanks for our health, home, and church family. Thank you for the unique talents and opportunities to minister You have given us. Lord, You've given me far more than I could ever deserve.

I ask You, Lord, to bless my family. Please continue to provide for us, as You always have. You've given us every dollar. "I've never seen the righteous forsaken or God's seed begging for bread." Lord, please continue to cover my baby girl with your protection. May she grow into a strong, God-fearing woman who stands for You in all circumstances. May she live up to her name (Petra) by her faith being unshakable and unbreakable, like a "rock." I pray for my sister in Christ, who is struggling with anxiety as she faces uncertainty. Lord, Your Word says You are Jehovah Shalom, the God of peace. Please minister that to her. Father, for the members of our church family with terminal cancer, I pray that they will feel their spirits lifted and that You will pour Your healing power over them. God, You are "the same yesterday, today, and forever," and the God of Biblical miracles still heals today. Please extend Your healing hand.

However, in all these things, Lord, I pray as Jesus prayed, "not my will, but Yours be done." "Many are the plans in a man's heart, but it is the Lord's purpose that prevails." So, Lord, I ask that You give me a heart to willingly submit to Your plans and purposes for myself and all those around me.

I give You all praise and glory, for You alone are worthy.

In Jesus' name,
Amen

Mario Cuomo –
Former Governor of New York

Like many other Americans, I really first became acquainted with Governor Mario Cuomo when he gave a rousing speech before the Democratic National Convention in 1984. Governor Cuomo was elected as the fifty-second governor of New York State in 1982 and served in that capacity until 1996. The *Boston Globe* has called Cuomo "the nation's most gifted philosopher-politician."

The son of Italian immigrant parents, Mario graduated summa cum laude from St. John's University in 1953 where he continued on to also earn his law degree. In 1954, he married Matilda Raffa, with whom he would have five children. In 1975, then-New York Governor Carey appointed him to the position of secretary of state, and in 1978, he became New York's lieutenant governor.

As governor, he initiated a 20 percent tax cut—the largest in the state's history. He also signed the first major ethics law for public officials. The state's mortality rates due to driving accidents decreased for seven consecutive years during his tenure, due to the first seat belt law in the country and also his tough stand on drunk drivers.

During his twelve-year tenure, he was able to balance the budget each year. His influence was much longer lasting than his years in office due to the fact that he appointed 112 judges.

His record earned for him wide acceptance from the populace, and twice he set New York records for the highest popular vote ever recorded in a New York statewide election.

Governor Mario M. Cuomo's favorite prayer:

> *We asked for strength that we might achieve,*
> *God made us weak that we might obey.*
> *We asked for health that we might do great things,*
> *He gave us infirmity that we might do better things.*
> *We asked for riches that we might be happy,*
> *We were given poverty that we might be wise.*
> *We asked for power that we might have the praise of men,*
> *We were given weakness that we might feel the need of God.*
> *We asked for all things that we might enjoy life,*
> *We were given life that we might enjoy all things.*
> *We received nothing that we asked for—all that we hoped for.*
> *And our prayers were answered.*
> *We were most blessed.*
>   *(Anonymous)*

Clive Cussler – Author

Clive Cussler was a flight engineer during the Korean War. After the war and before he became a world famous author, he won awards for writing and producing radio and TV commercials in Hollywood.

Cussler is an internationally acclaimed writer whose most famous works include *The Sea Hunters, Pacific Vortex, Mediterranean Caper, Iceberg, Raise the Titanic, Vixen 03, Night Probe, Deep Six, Cyclops, Treasure, Dragan, Sahara, Inca Gold, Shock Wave, Flood Tide,* and *Clive Cussler's Dirk Pitt Revealed.*

I was introduced to the works of Clive Cussler when he was on the required summer high school reading list for my son when he attended St. Ignatius High School in Cleveland, Ohio. My son and I both read Cussler's *Cyclops*. We both read Cussler, Pat Conroy, and others whose works were on this list. I wanted to make sure that Scott had read and digested his assignments. I would highly recommend this practice to other parents. I don't know if this routine was fully appreciated at the time, but I enjoyed both the reading and the discussions afterwards.

I found Cussler to be a great read, and I now find that we share a common experience—time spent at Lake Chautauqua in southwestern New York.

What a lot of people don't know about Clive Cussler is that he is an internationally recognized authority on shipwrecks. The following is a list of underwater finds with which he is associated: "the first submarine to sink a ship in battle, the Confederacy's *Hunley,* and its victim, the Union's *Housatonic*; the U-20, the U-boat that sank the *Lusitania*; the *Cumberland,* which was sunk by the famous ironclad, *Merrimack*; the renowned Confederate raider *Florida*; the navy airship, *Akron,* the Republic of Texas Navy warship, *Zavala,* found under a parking lot in Galveston, and the *Carpathia,* which sank almost six years to the day after plucking *Titanic's* survivors from the sea." The above list can be found on the website www.numa.net.

Clive and his wife Barbara have three children and two grandchildren.

☆   ☆   ☆

Clive Cussler sent us a "prayer for my tombstone."

"Dear Lord,

It was a great party while it lasted. I trust it will continue elsewhere."

Ann B. Davis –
"Alice" on the Brady Bunch

OK, let's see how good you are at playing Jeopardy. The category is TV characters from the '50s, '60s, and '70s. The answer is: "This actress played supporting roles in two popular TV sitcoms. In one show (1955-59) her character's name was Charmaine Schultz. For her part in this role, she won four Emmy nominations ('56, '57, '58, '59) and two Emmys ('58, '59). On the other show (1969-74), her character's name was Alice Nelson."

Give up? The actress's name is Ann B. Davis, whose nickname in the *Love that Bob/The Bob Cummings Show* was "Schultzy." In the second series, Ann played the feisty housekeeper "Alice" on the *The Brady Bunch*.

Few people know that Ann originally wanted to study to become a doctor while her twin sister, Harriet, was the one who was the first to study theater.

Ann never married and now spends a good amount of time in biblical studies and community involvement.

☆　　☆　　☆

Ann's favorite prayer is the biblical passage John 14:21:

> *"They who have my commandments and keep them are those who love me; and those who love me will be loved by my Father, and I will love them and reveal myself to them."*

Pete Dawkins –
Army Heisman Trophy winner

Because of his proximity to Detroit when growing up, Pete Dawkins had an early fascination with cars that led to his being a three-heat winner at the All-American Soap Box Derby. When he was eleven, this future Heisman Trophy winner was successfully treated for polio.

Pete attended West Point, where he served as brigade commander. He served as president of his class (1959), captain of the football team, and one of the top 5 percent academically in his class. Although he also played on the ice hockey and baseball teams, he excelled on the football field, and as stated earlier, he was awarded the 1958 Heisman Trophy (only the third cadet to ever be so honored).

As a Rhodes Scholar, he then spent three years at Oxford University, where he played on the rugby team.

Dawkins served two distinguished tours of duty in Vietnam and among his many awards were two Bronze Stars with "V" for valor.

Pete then taught at West Point before earning both his master's degree (1970) and doctoral degree (1979) from Princeton University.

Dawkins worked on the task force that changed the army's enrollment from a draft status to an all-volunteer unit.

In 1981, he received the rank of brigadier general. A year after his retirement (1983), he headed the fundraising effort for a Vietnam memorial.

Pete Dawkins then became as successful in the business field as he had been on the playing field and in his military career.

(If you are like me, you were trying to guess the other two cadets who won Heisman Trophies: "Mr. Inside" and "Mr. Outside," Doc Blanchard '45 and Glenn Davis '46.)

Pete Dawkins's favorite prayer:

> *Give us grateful hearts, our Father*
> *For all thy blessings.*
> *And make us ever mindful*
> *of the needs of others. Amen.*

Laraine Day – Movie Actress

Laraine Day's birth name was Laraine Johnson. She had a twin brother named Lamar. Laraine and Lamar were great-grandchildren of an important Mormon leader. When her family moved from Utah to Long Beach, California, Laraine received acting training from Elias Day, the manager of the Players Guild. And, in 1938, to honor her mentor, Laraine adopted Elias's surname.

Laraine first became familiar to the viewing public through her recurring role as Nurse Mary Lamont in seven Dr. Kildare films. When her studio became afraid that the public would typecast Day, scriptwriters had her character killed when she was hit by a truck in *Dr. Kildare's Wedding.*

Day and her first husband, James Ray Hendricks, adopted two daughters. Laraine later married baseball manager Leo Durocher, with whom she had a son. After her second divorce, Laraine married her present husband, Michael Grilikhes, in 1960. The couple has two daughters.

Although Laraine starred in many films, people will often remember her more for her involvement with Durocher's teams. From someone who originally knew nothing about the game, Laraine became known as the "First Lady of Baseball." She even wrote a book called *Day with the Giants* (1952) and had an interview show before each Giants home game.

☆   ☆   ☆

Laraine Day's favorite prayer is the biblical passage from John 3:16:

> *"For God so loved the world, that he gave his only Son, that everyone who believes in him may not perish, but may have eternal life."*

Dom DeLuise – Movie/TV Actor

It is very difficult to summarize Dom DeLuise's film credits in this small portrait that I am providing for each celebrity. I would recommend that for a more complete picture, you go on the Internet. If you do, I guarantee that you will be amazed at the list of film credits attached to Dom's name.

Dom DeLuise is associated with some classic film titles. He has appeared in *Fail Safe* (1964), *Blazing Saddles* (1974), *Silent Movie* (1976), *History of the World—Pt. 1* (1981), *Cannonball Run* (1980), *Best Little Whorehouse in Texas* (1982), *Robin Hood: Men in Tights* (1993), *Glass Bottom Boat* (1965), and *The End* (1978).

Dom is also an accomplished chef (he has written *Eat This* and *Eat This, Too*), has even performed with various opera companies through the years, and has authored several children's books. He and his wife, Carol, whom he married in 1965, have three sons (Peter, Michael, and David) who have all found success in show business. Dom, Carol, and the boys have appeared together in various media projects.

☆   ☆   ☆

Dom DeLuise sent the Serenity Prayer as his favorite reflection:

> *God, grant me the Serenity to accept the things I cannot change,*
> *Courage to change the things I can and*
> *Wisdom to know the difference.*

Phyllis Diller –
Comedienne

I recently read a book on levitation that I just couldn't put down!

That was my poor attempt at humor and my way of getting you ready for my portrait of Phyllis Diller.

I would think that along with Lucille Ball and Ellen DeGeneres, Phyllis Diller is one of our country's best-known and best-loved comediennes.

It seems like Phyllis has been around entertaining people forever, although she didn't begin her career until she was thirty-seven, after she raised her five children.

Phyllis has had a wide-ranging career. She has appeared on TV and in movies, she has recorded comedy albums, and has authored books. What many people don't realize is that she has appeared as a piano soloist with 100 symphony orchestras across the country. Few people also know that she writes her own routines.

Phyllis Diller has received countless awards for her many humanitarian efforts. And I don't think I'll be stretching it to say that Phyllis was really the first major star to acknowledge her use of cosmetic surgery.

The prayer that Phyllis Diller composed and sent:

<u>My Prayer</u>
On this happy day
I am thankful
For my blessings
And I pray
For renewed belief
In myself
And others
And hope
This bond of love
Will expand
To envelop
The entire universe.

Vince Dooley –
Georgia football coach and AD

From the year 1934 until 1976, the *Chicago Tribune* sponsored an exhibition game between the College All-Stars and the previous year's championship pro football team. Vince Dooley was an outstanding defensive back at Auburn University, and in 1954, he played with the All-Stars against the Detroit Lions.

In the '50s and '60s, Henry Althomeyer was the paper master for Naperville, Illinois. As a reward for their good work, each year, Henry would treat his paper carriers to a bus ride into Soldier Field to attend this football game. I was eight years old in 1954 and very well may have taken the bus in with my brother Bob and the rest of the news carriers to watch Vince Dooley play in this game. (Boy, do I now feel old!)

After graduating from Auburn, Dooley served two years in the Marine Corps. In 1964, at the age of thirty-one, Vince was named head coach at the University of Georgia, where he would compile a 201-77-10 record over the next twenty-five years. In 1980, Herschel Walker and the rest of the Georgia Bulldogs achieved a perfect 12-0 season, won the national championship, and earned Coach of the Year honors for Dooley.

After his coaching career, Vince continued on as Georgia's athletic director, a post he held from 1979 until 2004.

I taught history for thirty-three years. I am therefore very glad to get a prayer from Coach Dooley, who earned his master's degree in history in 1963.

(P.S. Just in case you are wondering, in that 1954 College All-Star game, the Detroit Lions with quarterback Bobby Layne defeated the collegians 31-6. I know that not from my own memory, but from my computer's memory.)

☆   ☆   ☆

Vince Dooley sent us this prayer invocation:

> *Dear Lord...Lead us by your spirit that we may be leaders, challenging others by our example to develop to the fullest our God-given talent.*

Dave Dravecky – Baseball pitcher

From the time he was a youngster, Dave's life revolved around baseball. In 1978, he was drafted out of Youngstown State in the twenty-first round by the Pittsburgh Pirates. A few months later, he married his high school sweetheart, Janice Rob.

By 1982, he was called up to the big leagues by the San Diego Padres. While with the Padres, he made the 1983 All-Star team and played in a World Series.

Dravecky was traded to the San Francisco Giants in 1987. The next year, doctors discovered cancer in his pitching arm, his left, and consequently removed half of his deltoid muscle.

Few people ever thought that Dave would pitch again. So, sports fans were amazed and inspired by his August 10, 1989 victory over the Cincinnati Reds in his first game back from his cancer surgery. Then, tragically, in his very next outing against the Montreal Expos, the bone in his pitching arm shattered. It was to break again just two months later while the Giants were celebrating their National League Championship Series over the Cubs. As a result, Dravecky had to retire from the game he loved in 1989.

Moreover, after three operations, doctors had to amputate his left arm, shoulder blade, and the left side of Dave's collarbone. Whereas many people would have, as a result, resorted to a life of negativity, misery, and bitterness, Dave and his wife Jan formed an organization called Outreach of Hope Ministries to help others who faced the same anxieties of cancer and amputation.

After his retirement from baseball, Dave wrote several books including:
-   *When You Can't Come Back* (written with his wife)
-   *The Worth of a Man*
-   *Play Ball*
-   *Do Not Lose Heart* (written with his wife and with Steve Halliday)

Dave and Jan have two children. Beside his writing, and his Outreach Ministries program, Dravecky is very active as an inspirational speaker.

Dave sent me this beautiful prayer for the book:

Dear Lord,

*Being healthy gives me a sense of being invincible—
but nothing blows that feeling out of the water more
quickly than being faced with some kind of affliction
or suffering. Whether I or someone I know is suffering,
affliction is a rude awakening to the fact that life is
short and each one of us is wasting away. Lord, it's
times like this that really cause me to think about the
things in life that are most important.*

*During this time of uncertainty, I find myself asking
questions I've rarely asked before. After all, there never
was a need to ask such questions; I had everything under
control. Everything was going great, just as I planned.
But now it's so different. I'm scared and quite frankly
I'm beginning to see a side of me that I don't much like.
Suffering does that to a person, I guess.*

*And yet, as I come to you in all my ugly sinfulness, I
now understand what the apostle Paul meant when
he said, "What a wretched man I am! Who will
rescue me from this body of death? Thanks be to God
through Jesus Christ our Lord!" I feel so much like
Paul, wretched and wondering who will rescue me.
Lord, I now know that if I place my trust in Jesus, it
is he who will rescue me from my sin and who will
give me the strength to endure this journey of life.
So, where does that leave me? I know this body won't*

last forever. Yet, Lord, I thank you that even in the midst of living with this broken-down body of mine, you have given HOPE! Yes, I know that outwardly, I am wasting away, but I also know that this pain and suffering have caused me to come face to face with my own ugly sinfulness…and that you have led me to Jesus, the One who rescues me from this body of death. He provides me with a HOPE that will last forever! Amen.

Denise Dufala –
Cleveland news anchor

Denise Dufala is one of Cleveland's most trusted and most beloved newscasters. Listening to Denise present the evening news is like hearing important stories being delivered by your best friend or family member. Denise is one of those people who looks like she definitely enjoys doing what she is doing.

She certainly has a grasp on what is happening in Cleveland because she grew up in one of its suburbs (North Olmsted), graduated from Ohio State, and has been reporting and anchoring news broadcasts for Cleveland news stations since 1986.

Apparently, Denise's enjoyment of life extends beyond her time in the newsroom. She loves antiques, ice skating, and singing as a member of her church choir. She has performed our national anthem before the games of all of Cleveland's professional sports teams.

Denise is especially fond of her position on the board of the Make-A-Wish Foundation.

☆　　☆　　☆

Regarding her favorite prayer, Denise Dufala writes: "Chuck, one of my favorite scriptures that helps me deal with the challenges of life is really the entire book of James. James was my father's name. In particular, I love 4:6-8:"

> *6 God opposes the proud, but gives grace to the humble.*
> *7 Submit yourselves therefore to God. Resist the devil,*
> *and he will flee from you.*
> *8 Draw near to God, and he will draw near to you.*
> *Cleanse your hands, you sinners, and purify your hearts,*
> *you double-minded.*

Father Virgil Elizondo –
Theology professor, Notre Dame

Our son, Scott, is an avid Notre Dame sports fan. So, when he reads this introduction for Father Virgil Elizondo, he will find Elizondo's dedication to his work in the Southwest not to be believed. You see, each week, the good father commutes to South Bend, Indiana, for his job as a visiting professor of theology at the university. And every weekend, he foregoes attendance at Fighting Irish football games to return to San Antonio to work on Catholic television.

Father Virgil's parents originally immigrated to the states from Mexico, and now their son is a leading authority on U.S./Latino religious thought. In between these two points in time, Virgil was ordained, earned his doctoral degree from Institut Catholique in Paris, was pastor from 1983 to 1995 of San Antonio's San Fernando Cathedral, and wrote ten books on the relationship between religion and culture.

In 1997, Father Elizondo received the Laetare Medal, the highest honor given by the University of Notre Dame. This award was established in 1883 and is given annually on Laetare Sunday to the Catholic "whose genius has ennobled the arts and sciences, illustrated the ideals of the Church, and enriched the heritage of humanity."

I can only imagine how proud Father Virgil's parents must be of the achievements of their son. San Antonians have an honored expression that they always "remember" a famous historical event that happened in their city. Rest assured that Father Elizondo has never forgotten his past or his people.

Father Elizondo's favorite prayer is:

The Memorare:

Remember, O most gracious Virgin Mary,
That never was it known that anyone who
    Fled to your protection,
    Implored your help, or
    Sought your intercession

Was left unaided.
Inspired with this confidence,
I fly unto you, O Virgin of virgins, my Mother;
To you, I come, before you, I stand, sinful and sorrowful;
O Mother of the Word Incarnate, despise not my petitions,
But in your mercy, hear and answer me.
    Amen.

Carl Erskine –
Dodgers pitcher

    I had the privilege of meeting Carl Erskine several years ago. Carl had come to Jamestown, New York, to help commemorate Brooklyn's return to professional baseball. The Cyclones were Brooklyn's representative in New York-Penn short-season league, and played their first game ever against the Jamestown Jammers. Carl played "Take Me Out to the Ball Game" on his harmonica during the seventh-inning stretch.

    But what I will always remember was Erskine's inspirational talk given the day before during a local fundraiser. Carl had the audience alternately laughing and crying. When asked what was the best pitch he ever threw, he responded, without hesitation: "The curve ball I threw in the dirt while warming up that prompted the pitching coach to bring in Ralph Branca to pitch to Bobby

Thomson in the 1951 playoff game" (Thomson ultimately hit a walk-off home run to send the Giants to the World Series).

Carl said that the medal his son won for swimming in the Special Olympic games meant more to him than any athletic award he had ever been given. And Carl Erskine did compile quite a record. He had a lifetime 122-78 record, which included two no-hitters.

After he retired, Erskine coached at Anderson College for twelve years, and has been a local community and business leader. I was honored to meet Carl and so glad he sent in a prayer.

☆   ☆   ☆

Carl Erskine's favorite prayer:

> "Lord, I don't pray for life to be easier, but for you to make me stronger."

Mike Eruzione –
Captain of the 1984 gold medal hockey team

Those people born between 1924 and 1964 most likely personally witnessed on radio or TV the "Miracle on Ice" the phrase that denotes the 1984 U.S. Men's Olympic Gold Medal performance at Lake Placid, New York. Those people born since

1964 most probably were introduced to the event through the 2003 movie, *Miracle,* which details the development of that team under the tutelage of coach Herb Brooks.

The "miracle" 4-3 victory over the Russians actually took place in a semi-final match-up. Not a lot of people realize that the "miracle" win wouldn't have meant as much historically had the U.S. not gone on to defeat Finland in the championship game. One of the main reasons the U.S. victory was so unexpected is that the U.S. squad had been trounced 10-3 by the Russians in an exhibition match.

Mike Eruzione excelled in baseball and football as well as hockey while he was in high school. He then went on to lead Boston University to four Eastern College hockey championships. Eruzione was an ECAC all-star three years and also all-New England three years. Before becoming a member of the famous 1984 Olympic team, Mike played for the 1975 and 1976 U.S. national teams.

Not only was Mike Eruzione the captain of the U.S. Olympic team, but he scored the winning goal against the Russians.

Mike never played for any major professional hockey team. After the Olympics, he went into broadcasting and the lecture circuit.

Mike has returned to his alma mater where he is Director of Development for Athletics. He and his wife, Donna, have three children.

Mike writes that his favorite prayer is the Lord's Prayer. He said that he also likes when the prayer is put to song—a song he used to sing when he was in high school glee club:

<u>The Lord's Prayer</u>
(Matthew 6:9-13 & Luke 11:2-4)
9v. Our Father, who art in Heaven,
Hallowed be thy name.
10v. Thy kingdom come, thy will be done,
On earth as it is in Heaven.
11v. Give us this day our daily bread
12v. And forgive us our trespasses
13v. As we forgive those who trespass against us.
And lead us not into temptation,
But deliver us from evil.
For thine is the kingdom, and the power, and the glory, forever.
Amen.

Gerry Faust –
Notre Dame and Akron University football coach

In 2004, Gerry Faust was inducted as a coach into the High School Athletic Hall of Fame. After lettering for three years as a quarterback for the University of Dayton, Faust started his coaching career as an assistant coach for two years at his alma mater, Chaminade High School in Dayton, Ohio.

Gerry then became head coach for twenty-one years at Cincinnati's Archbishop Moeller High School. During his tenure, Coach Faust achieved an amazing 174-17-2 record; his teams recorded nine undefeated seasons; and from 1972 to 1978, Moeller had a fifty-three regular game win streak. The news media gave the Faust-coached Moeller teams four national championships. Gerry was named Ohio Coach of the Year six times and national Coach of the Year twice.

The University of Notre Dame rewarded Faust's high school record by naming him to replace Dan Devine as the twenty-fourth head coach of the Fighting Irish. Coach Faust compiled a 30-26-1 record and two bowl appearances in five seasons at Notre Dame. Although his teams posted a winning percentage, the Irish demanded an even greater measure of perfection. Unfortunately, Gerry's tenure at Notre Dame was sandwiched in between two Notre Dame coaches (Devine and Holtz) who brought national championships to the school.

Coach Faust then was hired by the University of Akron to head their football program. Gerry's teams posted a 30-26-1 record, but Coach's major accomplishment was to bring Akron football from Division 1-AA up to Division 1-A where the competition was much stiffer.

Since retiring from coaching in 1995 Coach Faust has authored two books: *The Golden Dream* and *Tales from the Notre Dame Sideline*.

Gerry now spends his time as a motivational speaker and loving grandfather. His caring nature is revealed in the 2004 commencement address that he delivered to the University of Dayton's law school. In his talk, Coach Faust gave his "four guiding principles to happiness and successful living:"
- Have strong faith
- Have a great love for your family
- Have peace of mind
- Learn to give in life

In a telephone conversation, Coach Faust related that he had two favorite prayers. The first was the Memorare. When Gerry was in the sixth grade he played center for Our Lady of Mercy CYO football team. Faust vividly remembers the morning of the CYO championship game when their eighth grade captain Russ Sweetman led the team in the recitation of the Memorare. Our Lady of Mercy went on to upset St. Joseph Orphanage in that title game and the Memorare has been Coach Faust's favorite prayer ever since.

The Memorare

Remember, O most Gracious Virgin Mary,
that never was it known that anyone who
fled to they protection,
implored thy help, and
sought thy intercession, was left unaided.
Inspired with this confidence, i fly unto thee,
O Virgin of Virgins, my Mother;
To thee I come, before thee I stand, sinful and sorrowful.
O Mother of the Word Incarnate!
despise not my petitions, but in thy mercy
hear and answer me. Amen.

Faust's second-favorite form of prayer is the recitation of the "rosary." Beads are usually held to count a series of prayers basically consisting of five meditations around a particular daily theme. In modern times, these themes include mysteries of the church that are identified as Joyful (recited on Mondays and Saturdays); Luminous (recited on Thursdays), Sorrowful (recited on Tuesdays and Fridays), and Glorious (recited on Wednesdays and Sundays). During the meditation on each theme, one is to pray five sets consisting of an "Our Father" followed by ten (a decade) "Hail Marys." The rosary is begun with the recitation of the Apostles' Creed and is ended with the prayer called "Hail, Holy Queen." Coach Faust often recites the rosary on his way to appointments and speaking engagements. Gerry related that he is probably the only person ever pulled over by a police officer for erratic driving due to concentrating on the saying of the rosary.

General Tommy Franks – U.S. general/Iraqi War

A number of years ago, there was a commercial with featured Certs breath mints. The commercial asserted (pun intended) that Certs was both a breath mint and a candy mint. The jingle stated Certs was "Two, two, two mints in one!

Well, when I read about General Tommy Franks, I get the idea that he too has two distinct aspects to his personality.

1. On the one hand, he is a tough soldier who was wounded three times in Vietnam and who served in the Gulf War. He moved steadily up the military ranks and became a general in the year 2000. At that time, he was named Commander-in-Chief of United States Central Command, which placed him in charge of a twenty-five-country area which included the Middle East. General Franks led the assault on the Taliban in Afghanistan, commanded

the 2003 invasion of Iraq, and then became the temporary military governor of Iraq. He retired on July 7, 2003.

As a result of his military performance, he earned three Purple Hearts, four Legion of Merit Awards, and three Bronze Stars with Valor. After his retirement, President George W. Bush honored him with the Presidential Medal of Freedom.

2. On the other hand, the general is the gentle man who his grandchildren call "Pooh" after the storybook bear character. He is the man who has been quoted as saying that, "No one hates war like a soldier hates war." He is the man who is listed in the official military biography, not as Thomas or Tom, but as General Tommy Franks. He is the intelligent, thoughtful man who earned a B.A. from the University of Texas and an M.A. from Shippensburg University. He is a devoted husband, married to his wife Cathy since 1969. They have one daughter, Jacqy.

My wife and I questioned the process by which our administration invaded Iraq. But we were always confident in the ability of our soldiers and General Franks. We were confident that he had the military courage, ability, and strength, as well as the wisdom and compassion to liberate the country from the rule of Saddam Hussein, all the while fulfilling his mission as effectively as possible.

It is interesting to note that General Franks was two years ahead of classmate Laura Bush in high school in Midland, Texas.

General Franks wrote this note to accompany his prayer response:

"For almost four decades, I've prayed for strength to wear the 'whole armor of God' as described in Ephesians 6, verses 10-18:"

> *"Finally, be strong in the Lord and in the strength of his power. Put on the whole armor of God, so that*

you may be able to stand against the wiles of the devil. For our struggle is not against enemies of blood and flesh, but against the rulers, against the authorities, against the cosmic powers of this present darkness, against the spiritual forces of evil in the heavenly places. Therefore, take up the whole armor of God, so that you may be able to withstand on that evil day, and having done everything, to stand firm. Stand therefore, and fasten the belt of truth around your waist, and put on the breastplate of righteousness. As shoes for your feet, put on whatever will make you ready to proclaim the gospel of peace. With all of these, take the shield of faith, with which you will be able to quench all the flaming arrows of the evil one. Take the helmet of salvation, and the sword of the Spirit, which is the word of God. Pray in the Spirit at all times in every prayer and supplication. To that end, keep alert and always persevere in supplication for all the saints."

Father Joseph Girzone – Author of "Joshua" series

I feel a lot of empathy for Father Joseph Girzone, and I'll tell you why after I give you a little of his background.

Joseph graduated from St. Bonaventure University (Olean, New York) which is just a forty-five-minute drive from our home here on Chautauqua Lake. Girzone was ordained into the priesthood in 1955 and spent the next nine years as a high school teacher. Then, for the next seventeen years, he served as pastor at a succession of churches in the Pennsylvania and New York area. When Father Girzone turned fifty, his health started to deteriorate and his doctor strongly advised him to retire from the stresses of parish life.

It was this occasion that prompted Girzone to become a full-time author in order not to be a financial burden on his diocese.

Father Girzone has written more than twenty books. However, the books for which he has become famous form his *Joshua* series. Each *Joshua* book tells the story of the impact the return of Jesus Christ (Joshua) has on a particular location in modern society.

After the completion of his first *Joshua* book, Girzone found it quite difficult to find a publisher willing to print his effort. Father Girzone obviously had a lot of gumption, for he decided to print his own work. In order to do this, he had to become familiar with computers. He was so successful in this endeavor that he even became a leading area salesman for Olivetti computers!

I, too, have had difficulty in finding a publisher for my work. I credit Father Girzone as one of many who have inspired me and convinced me that I could successfully publish this *Book of Prayers*.

Father Girzone sent a reply not unlike a response I would expect to come from his character, Joshua. The author/priest wrote that my letter made him realize that he doesn't have a favorite prayer.

"I just talk to God or the Blessed Mother or one of my favorite saints at various times during the day and try to realize God's presence all day long."

Archie Griffin –
Only two-time Heisman Trophy winner

In 2004, the Ohio State Buckeyes named Archie Griffin as president and CEO of their alumni association. It is impossible for me to imagine a more appropriate choice, for no alumnus is a better representative for their school, has set a higher standard of excellence, and is a more charismatic leader. Here are but a few of Griffin's achievements during his tenure (1972 to 1975) at Ohio State:

- Only two-time Heisman Trophy winner
- OSU was 40-5-1 during his four years
- OSU won Big 10 titles each of his four years
- Only player to ever start four Rose Bowls
- One of only two players (Indiana's Anthony Thompson '88-'89 was the other) to be awarded consecutive Big 10 MVP awards
- Holds NCAA record for most consecutive (thirty-one) 100-yard rushing games

- Scored 26 touchdowns and ran for 5,589 yards during his collegiate career
- Three-time first team All American
- First OSU athlete to have his number (45) retired
- Graduated from OSU a quarter early with a degree in industrial relations.

What is as impressive to me about Archie Griffin is that he has continued his standard of excellence even after his collegiate and NFL pro (eight years with the Cincinnati Bengals) ended. Griffin was awarded the NCAA Silver Anniversary Award given to a very select number of former athletes who have distinguished themselves in the twenty-five years after completing their collegiate careers.

Archie and his wife, Bonita, have three children: Anthony, Andre, and Adam.

Archie Griffin's favorite prayer is the Lord's Prayer (Mt. 6:9-13 & Luke 11:2-4):

> *Our Father, Who art in heaven, hallowed by Thy name. Thy kingdom come, Thy will be done on earth, as it is in heaven.*
>
> *Give us this day our daily bread, and forgive us our trespasses, as we forgive those who trespass against us, and lead us not into temptation, but deliver us from evil.*
>
> *For thine is the kingdom, and the power, and the glory, forever. Amen.*

Karolyn Grimes –
Played "Zuzu" in *It's a Wonderful Life*

"Dear Father, I'm not a praying man, but if you're up there and you can hear me, show me the way. I'm at the end of my rope. Show me the way, oh God."

"George Bailey" (as played by Jimmy Stewart) in It's a Wonderful Life (1946 film produced and directed by Frank Capra).

"Frankly Scarlett, I don't give a damn."

Most film buffs immediately can associate this movie line with Clark Gable in the classic movie, *Gone With the Wind.* But few people can identify the actress credited with the following famous lines from an equally famous movie *It's a Wonderful Life*: "Each time a bell rings, an angel gets his wings!" Those lines were spoken in 1946 by a little six-year-old actress, Karolyn Grimes, who was playing the part of "Zuzu" in the film.

Up to the point when Karolyn played that part in the movie, she had indeed herself lived a wonderful life. To that point in her young life, she had been in four films and would ultimately end up with roles in sixteen movies featuring the likes of movie greats John Wayne, Betty Grable, Cary Grant, Bing Crosby, and Loretta Young.

However, Karolyn—unlike Shirley Temple to whom she was sometimes compared—would have her movie career cut short by tragedy. Karolyn's mother died of early-onset Alzheimer's and her father was killed in a car crash. Subsequently Karolyn, an only child, was sent by the courts to live with a family in Osceola, Missouri, far from the lights of Hollywood.

Her first marriage ended in divorce. Subsequently, her ex-husband was killed two years later in a hunting accident. Her second husband died of lung cancer. The youngest child of her blended family of seven children committed suicide. (Still thinking you're having a bad day?)

I e-mailed Karolyn and asked her if she knew the origins of the name "Zuzu," the famous character who said those memorable lines in that epic Christmas tale. Little did I know what a wonderful anecdotal response I would receive from Karolyn:

"The original story of *IAWL* came from a Christmas card written by Philip Van Dorenstern. Eventually, it became a book titled *The Greatest Gift*. When Frank Capra got this project, he got some other screenwriters involved and had them write screen adaptations. One of the people he used was a man named Clifford Odette. He is the man who came up with the name. Capra ended up using the three different scripts along with his own ideas to come up with his final version.

Around the early 1900s, there was a product called Zuzu's Ginger Snaps made by the National Biscuit Company. Today that company is Nabisco. It featured a little clown called Zuzu on all its advertising.

George Bailey comes home after he finds that he is alive again and he runs upstairs to see his children. I run out the door and he exclaims 'Zuzu, my little gingersnap!'"

Karolyn Grimes sent me a beautiful e-mail that described her favorite prayer:

"The prayer that has sustained me throughout the years of my life is simply the 23rd Psalm. I first heard the prayer when Cary Grant recited it to me during the movie *The Bishop's Wife*. It has become my mantra since those early days of my life. He talked about the meaning of the verse, and little did I know the adversity that I would face throughout my life and still do. 'The Lord is my shepherd; I shall not want' has encouraged me to ask for help when needed and to give thanks when needed as well. He guides me through the 'still waters' and when crisis hits, he guides me through 'the valley of death.' He gives me the strength to fear no evil and gives me the promise of a wonderful eternity."

The 23rd Psalm
The Lord is my shepherd; I shall not want.
He makes me lie down in green pastures,
He leads me beside the still waters.
He restores my soul.
He leads me in right paths for his name's sake.
Even though I walk through the darkest valley,
I will fear no evil; for you are with me.
Your rod and your staff, they comfort me.
You prepare a table before me in the presence of mine enemies.
You anoint my head with oil, my cup overflows.
Surely goodness and mercy shall follow me all the days of my life.
And I will dwell in the house of the Lord my whole life long.

Ioan Gruffudd – Welsh actor

In 1869, in upstate New York, Stub Newell and his brother-in-law, George Hull, initiated the hoax of the Cardiff Giant. The year before, the two had a ten-and-a-half-foot-tall giant carved out of gypsum and had it buried in a marsh in back of Newell's farm in Cardiff, New York. The next year (1869), Newell hired a crew to dig a well in that exact location and "voila!" The workers came upon the "petrified humanoid" and the hoax was born. So many people paid to view the figure that Barnum and Bailey created another fake Cardiff giant out of wood. This second figure, believe it or not, actually attracted more spectators that the original! Eventually, scientists were able to convince the public that the giant was man-made and only a few years rather than a thousand years old. The fake Cardiff giant now resides in a museum in Cooperstown, New York.

Now, there is a real, living Cardiff giant. This man is an actor and is proving to be a "giant" in the entertainment industry. His name is Ioan Gruffudd and he is from the real, legitimate, Cardiff, Wales (not like Cardiff, New York, whose name was formed by stretching the name of the town's founder, a Mr. Car).

Ioan won his first role at the age of fourteen on a Welsh soap opera, *People of the Valley*. After he graduated from the Royal Academy of Dramatic Arts, he acted in the 1997 film *Wilde*. That same year he landed the role of Officer Lowe in the blockbuster movie, *Titanic.* More recently, he starred as Lancelot in *King Arthur* (2004) and as Reed Richards, AKA, Mr. Fantastic, in the 2005 film *Fantastic Four.*

On the TV screen, Ioan started to build equally impressive credentials for his starring roles in *Poldark* (1996),the mini-series *Hornblower* (1997-2003), *Great Expectations* (1999), and *The Miracle Maker* (2000).

Gruffudd is very close to his parents, Peter and Gillian, as well as his brother and sister. He is also proud of his Welsh heritage and asked that his prayer first be printed in his native Welsh language. Actually, Ioan's mother, Mrs. Gill Gruffudd, responded for her son and wrote that the prayer is usually sung: "The prayer is an adaptation by W. Owen Evans (1864-1936) of the first verse of a hymn by Charles Wesley (1707-1788), 'Gentle Jesus.' I include my translation of the Welsh verse as it stands, as it isn't an exact translation of the original English verse by Wesley."

> *Iesu tirion, gwel yn awr*
> *Blentyn bach yn ply gu lawr;*
> *Wrth fy ngwendid trugarha*
> *Paid a'm gwrthod, Iesu da. Amen.*

> *Gentle Jesus, see now*
> *A small child kneeling*
> *Be merciful toward my weakness*
> *Don't reject me, good Jesus. Amen*

Janet Guthrie –
First Woman driver in the Indy 500

As of 2007, there were only five women to have ever raced in the Indianapolis 500. Most recently, Milka Duno finished 31st in her first Indy 500 race (2007). Danica Patrick competed in the last three Indy 500s (2005-2007). Sarah Fisher drove entries from 2000 to 2004 and again in 2007. Prior to Sarah, Lyn St. James raced at the Brickyard from 1992 to 1997, and again in 2000. But the very first woman representative at the Indy 500 was Janet Guthrie, who raced there from 1977 to 1979. It was more than appropriate that Janet broke the ice for women in this event.

Janet's racing accomplishments should be magnified because, as a woman and a rookie, she most often had to settle for cars that were only put in the race to fill out the field.

Guthrie's thrill for speed was grounded on a solid basis. She graduated from the University of Michigan with a degree in physics. And her spirit of adventure came early. At the age of seventeen, she earned her pilot's license. She also was one of the first women astronaut candidates.

Janet began auto racing in 1963, and eventually established many firsts for women in this sport. In 1976, she was the first to compete in a NASCAR Winston Cup event (earlier, when the racing circuit was called Strictly Stock, Louise Smith raced in a NASCAR event in 1949).

In 1977, Janet was the first woman to compete at Daytona, the same year she broke the sex barrier at Indy. Her qualifying speed of 188.403 earned her the twenty-sixth position at the start of the 1977 Indy 500. But, engine trouble forced her out of the race and she finished twenty-ninth. The next year, she qualified for fifteenth position and finished in ninth place. Her third and final year at the Brickyard, she started fourteenth but finished thirty-fourth.

Janet was inducted into the Women's Sports Hall of Fame in 1980 and her helmet and driver's suit are in the Smithsonian Museum. In 2005, her autobiography—*Janet Guthrie: A Life at Full Throttle*—was published. The old expression is "You can't judge a book by its cover." In Janet's case, the cover or, more specifically, the title, covers its subject perfectly.

Not only has Janet Guthrie been a role model for women racers, but her perseverance in getting her writing into book form has inspired this author as well. From a very young age, Janet wrote down her thoughts in journal form. In 1983, she started using an old Corona to type up these journals. It was twenty-two years before Janet finished and the book was published. My frustrations at publication pale in comparison to Guthrie's.

Janet married Warren Levine in 1989. Warren's résumé is also impressive. He was a pilot for American Airlines for twenty-seven years without taking a single sick day. He also was a talented classical pianist. Levine died of a heart attack on December 30, 2006.

When Janet wrote me her favorite prayer, she explained, "In my family (brothers, sisters, spouses, and my mother), there are various forms of belief, but the practice of saying grace before meals is important to us all. So we have adopted the simplest possible form:

"For what we are about to receive, we are truly thankful."'

Mike Hargrove –
Baseball player/manager

Can you identify each of the major leaguers associated with the following nicknames: the Splendid Splinter, Big Train, Oil Can, Big Unit, the Georgia Peach, Hammerin' Hank, Bye-bye, the Rocket, or Catfish? (The answers are at the end of this introduction.) Mike Hargrove is one of a number of major leaguers who are famous for the nicknames they acquired during their big league career. Hargrove was known as "the Human Rain Delay" for the calculated routine of adjustments he went through before each pitch.

Mike was a three-sport letterman (baseball, basketball, and football) at Northwest Oklahoma. It was only after the twenty-fourth round that the Texas Rangers drafted Mike in 1972. Yet, after just two years, he made his debut with the parent club and was named the American League's Rookie of the Year. That year, 1974, he batted .323 with fourteen doubles, ten home runs, and fifty-six RBI's. In his eleven-year career, which saw Mike play for the Padres and Indians, he compiled a .290 average with 80 home runs and 686 RBI's in 1,666 total games.

Since his playing days, Mike has had managerial stints with Cleveland, Baltimore, and Seattle. He was named American League Manager of the Year in 1993 (*USA Today*) and in 1995 (*Sporting News*). In his nine years with Cleveland, the Indians won five consecutive American League Central Division titles and two American League Championships.

Mike and his charming wife Sharon have five children (Kimberly, Melissa, Pamela, Andrew, and Cynthia). In 1989, Sharon wrote a book called *Safe at Home: A Baseball Wife's Story*.

Answers to nicknames, in order presented above: Ted Williams (the Splendid Splinter), Walter Johnson (Big Train), Dennis Boyd (Oil Can), Randy Johnson (Big Unit), Ty Cobb (the Georgia Peach), Hank Aaron (Hammerin' Hank), Steve Balboni (Bye-bye), Roger Clemens (the Rocket), and Jim Hunter (Catfish).

This prayer was sent to Mike from his sister after the death of their mother. It has become a favorite, and Mike and his sister end each visit with "I Wish You Enough."

I Wish You Enough

I wish you enough sun to keep your attitude bright.
I wish you enough rain to appreciate the sun more.
I wish you enough happiness to keep your spirit alive.
I wish you enough pain so that the smallest joys in life appear much bigger.
I wish you enough gain to satisfy your wanting.
I wish you enough loss to appreciate all that you possess.
I wish you enough "Hello's" to get you through the final "Good-bye."

Mike's favorite Bible verse is Romans 8:28:

> *"We know that all things work together for good for those who love God, who are called according to his purpose."*

Brian Harper – Baseball catcher

Brian Harper was drafted out of high school in the fourth round of the 1977 draft by the California Angels. I believe Brian is a true study in patience because, although he played eighteen years of professional ball (twelve years in the majors), he did not become a starter until 1989. By this time he was thirty years old, and he was playing for his sixth different major league team, the Minnesota Twins. Brian made excellent use of his time as a starter, as illustrated by the following statistics. Calf and wrist injuries forced him to retire in 1995.

- Brian had a career major league batting average of .295. In 1990, Brian established the fifth all-time longest hitting streak (twenty-five games) among major league catchers. (OK, I know you by now, and you want me to list the four catchers who had longer hitting streaks. Here they are: Benito Santiago (34 games), Sandy Alomar Jr. (30 games), and John Flaherty and Gabby Hartnett (26 games each).

- Brian hit over .300 in four out of six years he was with the Twins.
- Brian played in two different World Series (with the Cardinals in 1985, and the Twins in 1991).
- Brian's .391 batting average for the Twins in the 1991 World Series led his team.

Brian earned the reputation as being a contact hitter and a very tough player to strike out. In fact, he only struck out 188 times in more than 3,300 career at bats. Someone with such a low strike-out rate usually will have a very high number of walks. However, Brian had even fewer walks (133) than strikeouts!

After his career in the majors, Harper coached high school baseball in Scottsdale, Arizona, and in 2002, became the manager of the Mesa Angels rookie team.

Brian wrote that the biblical passage from John 17:21, 23 was his favorite prayer:

> *"I pray that all of them may be one, Father, just as you are in me and I am in you....I in them and you in me. May they be brought to complete unity to let the world know that you sent me and have loved them."*

Brian concluded his note with the words, "Lord bring us to unity in Love!"

Mother Dolores Hart –
Movie star; Mother Superior

The story of Dolores Hart is a very unusual one. She was born to show business parents and her birth name was Dolores Hicks. She was not raised a Catholic, but this precocious girl at the age of ten made her wishes known to convert to this religion.

When Dolores was not even twenty years old, she starred in Elvis Presley's first two films: *Loving You* (1957) and *King Creole* (1958). In the first of these films, she illustrated her musical ability by singing two songs ("Dancing on a Dime" and "Detour"). In 1959, Dolores starred in the Broadway play, "The Pleasure of His Company."

Hart's next big film was with Yvette Mimieux and Connie Francis in *Where the Boys Are* (1960). In 1961, she was in the movie *Francis of Assisi,* and in 1962, she was the title character in a story of the Holocaust called *Lisa.* These two films were to have a significant impact on Dolores's future lifestyle.

By this time in her career, Dolores was starting to be compared to the actress Grace Kelly. In 1956, the lovely Ms. Kelly left Hollywood to become royalty in Monaco. Hart's comparison with the life of Ms. Kelly was to become even more appropriate when in 1963, she also chose to leave Hollywood for another lifestyle. However, Dolores's departure was to the Benedictine Abby of Regina Laudis in Connecticut. There she became a nun and took on the name of Sister Judith. When she made her final vows in 1970, she made her profession as Sister Dolores.

Sister Dolores has been at Regina Laudis since she left Hollywood. She has been an inspiration as someone who has put a higher value on a life of spiritual focus over one focused on material attention and personal wealth.

☆　　☆　　☆

In Mother Dolores Hart's response to my prayer request letter, she describes the mode of "sacred prayer that has been most meaningful in my contemplative life, now of forty years."

"You may know that our Abbatial Community of Contemplative Nuns follows the Rule of Saint Benedict. Seven times a day and once in the middle of the night, we chant, as prayer, the Divine Office which is an arrangement of the Psalms set forth by Saint Benedict more than 1,500 years ago. Since this Abbey's founding, we have held to the tradition of the Chant in Latin. Although a communal expression, Gregorian Chant is also a personal experience of the praise of God for each member of our Community."

Ernie Harwell –
Announcer for the Detroit Tigers

Tongue-tied as a youngster, Ernie Harwell went on in 1981 to become only the fifth broadcaster to ever be inducted into the Baseball Hall of Fame.

Because his family experienced particularly hard times, Ernie and his two brothers had jobs early on. Ernie had a paper route. (One of his customers was Margaret Mitchell!) At the age of sixteen, he became a reporter for *The Sporting News* and soon after, the *Atlanta Constitution*.

Ernie met his wife, Lulu, when they were both students at Emory University. During his time as a marine in WWII, Harwell wrote for the corps newspaper, *Leatherneck*.

Ernie started doing play-by-play for the minor league Atlanta Crackers. He got paid $25 per game, plus a case (twenty-five boxes to a case) of Wheaties from that team's sponsor every time a Cracker player hit a home run. Harwell became the only announcer traded for a player when the Dodgers won Ernie's services by exchanging Brooklyn farmhand Cliff Draper for him. Ernie broadcast games for the Dodgers, Giants, Orioles, and then finally landed with the Detroit Tigers in 1960.

People are surprised to know that Harwell, besides writing several sports books, has composed sixty-six songs that have been recorded by various artists.

During the first broadcast of each year, Ernie would recite the following lines from the biblical Song of Solomon:

> *For the winter is past,*
> *The rain is over and gone;*
> *The flowers appear on the earth;*
> *The time of the song of the birds has come,*
> *And the voice of the turtle is heard in our land.*

Ernie Harwell sent me the invocation he read at the request of Ted Williams at one of his Hall of Fame banquets in February of 2000:

"Lord, we feel your presence here tonight. You are always with us. You are our God of life and our victory over death. In life, you are completely in charge—even in the sometimes inconsequential.

"You are the God of strikeouts and home runs, of errors and brilliant catches, or jeers and cheers. Most of all, you are the God of the final score. We thank you that our final score, regardless of strikeouts or mishaps, can be our salvation through your son, Jesus Christ. In his name, we ask you to bless this food tonight."

Father Edward Hays – Religious author/specialty is prayer

Al Toejnes, a former college classmate and friend, recommended that I send Father Edward Hays a prayer request letter. I have since discovered that Father Hays and I share a common tie. We both graduated from Conception Seminary College, although Ed's commencement ceremonies preceded my 1968 graduation by fourteen years.

Hays spent his first thirteen years as a priest in parish life. After a sabbatical, he was invited by his archbishop to found a diocesan house of prayer. Father Hays accepted the challenge and formed "Shantiyanam," whose name in Sanskrit means "forest of peace." Shantiyanam is located in Easton, Kansas, less than an hour's drive northwest of Kansas City.

Not only has Father Hays written eighteen books on prayer and spirituality, he also does his own illustrations either in pen and ink on in watercolor.

In reading up on Father Hays and his writings, I think I am especially impressed by the idea that he expressed to Anita McSorley in an interview that appeared in the *St. Anthony Messenger* (12/30/04). Hays noted "that individuals tend to experience the God they believe in." So, if we believe in a God who's only in heaven, we might not now appreciate and pray to God who is with us in our daily lives.

☆   ☆   ☆

I found it interesting that, although Father Hays has perhaps written more about prayer than any other celebrity in this book, his prayer was the shortest but yet perhaps ultimately the most profound. He wrote simply:

"My favorite prayer is 'AMEN!'"

Michael Heaton – Columnist for the *Cleveland Plain Dealer*

I spent my thirty-three-year teaching career (1968-2002) in Cleveland, Ohio. Along the way, my wife and I became friends with Doug Dieken (see Foreword), the Browns' offensive tackle from 1971 to 1984. So I naturally paid more attention than normal to the reflections of the legendary *Cleveland Plain Dealer* sportswriter Chuck Heaton concerning the Browns' fortunes.

Chuck and his first wife Pat lived in Bay Village and had four girls (one of whom is a Dominican nun in Virginia) and one boy, Michael. Four years after Pat died in 1971, Chuck married CeCe Evers, to whom he has been married for more than thirty years. Michael has followed in his father's footsteps as a journalist, just not in the sports department, but as a feature writer. He has a column entitled "The Minister of Culture." Michael has won a number of awards for his writing, including best feature writer (2003). In addition, he has authored three books and is working on a novel called *Everything Takes Forever.*

Michael is married and has three daughters. His sister Patricia ("Patty") is the Hollywood actress especially famous for her role as Debra Barone on *Everybody Loves Raymond.*

Michael Heaton's favorite prayer:

> *Father, we thank you for the night*
> *and the pleasant morning light,*
> *For the rest and food and loving care*
> *and all that makes the world so fair.*
> *Help us to do the things we should,*
> *to be to others kind and good.*
> *In all we do in work and play,*
> *to grow more loving every day.*
> *Amen.*

Bunny Hoest –
Cartoonist ("Lockhorns")

Bunny Hoest's father was a doctor. From the magazines that were in his outer office, Bunny got an early interest in cartoons. She went on to earn her B.A. in English and an M.A. in education. Bunny met cartoonist Bill Hoest in 1972 at a local tennis tournament, and the two collaborated in producing a collection of the best of *The Lockhorns*, a strip that Bill had started in 1968. The name *Lockhorns* had been shortened from the original more local title *The Lockhorns of Levittown*, named after a housing development on Long Island.

Bunny and Bill were married in 1973. Bunny started to work with her husband on his various cartoon creations that included *Bumper Snickers* (1974), *Agatha Crumm* (1977), *Laugh Parade* (1982), *Howard Huge* (1981), and finally, *What a Guy!* (1987).

After her husband died of cancer in 1988, Bunny took over the features with the help of cartoonist John Reiner. When Bunny remarried (Dr. Walter Carpenter), she dropped *Agatha Crumm*, *What a Guy!*, and *Bumper Snickers*.

The Lockhorns currently is featured in 500 newspapers worldwide. Hoest was honored by having *Howard Huge* featured on the Armed Forces Task Force Calendar for 2004 that had a distribution of 600,000.

Can you remember the names of the couple featured in the Lockhorns? They are Leroy and Loretta. And the dog,

Howard Huge, is patterned after the Hoests' St. Bernard named Euripedes.

☆　　☆　　☆

In response to our prayer request letter, Bunny Hoest wrote:

"At our family gatherings, we end by singing 'God Bless America.' It is our heartfelt expression of humility and gratitude for the blessings of this great land.

God bless America, land that I love.
Stand beside her and guide her,
Through the night with a light from above.
From the mountains, to the prairies,
To the ocean white with foam.
God bless America, my home sweet home,
God bless America, my home sweet home.
With thanks to Irving Berlin, and to you, Chuck for asking."

Lou Holtz –
ND and South Carolina football coach

Lou Holtz is one of the most entertaining and inspirational speakers around. He is known for his self-deprecating humor. I have always gotten a kick out of hearing Lou build up his next football opponent—no matter how terrible that team's record might be.

I've always loved Coach Holtz because I was a career history teacher and Lou majored in history during his days at Kent State University. I also liked the fact that he set a list of goals for himself in a wide variety of fields of endeavor.

Lou compiled a long list of coaching credentials that included head coaching stints at the College of William and Mary, North Carolina State, the University of Minnesota, Notre Dame University, and finally, the University of South Carolina.

Lou will probably be best remembered for taking his 1988 Fighting Irish team to victory in the National Championship over my West Virginia Mountaineers.

Here is Coach Holtz's favorite prayer that he used in order to help himself and his players put the game they played into perspective:

> *Dear Lord,*
> *We pray that you open our eyes to see the talents and opportunities you have bestowed upon us, our ears to hear and heed the instructions from our coaches, our minds that we perceive challenges as nothing more than opportunities, our mouths to praise other people, and our hearts to love and appreciate the goodness in other people, so that when this season is successfully completed we can come to you on bended knees and humbly say, we have done your will.*

Lou also sent a second prayer that I thought should be included:

"This is the beginning of a new day. God has given me this day to use as I will. I can waste it—or use it for good, but what I do today is important, because I am exchanging a day of my life for it! When tomorrow comes, this day will be gone forever, leaving in its place something that I have traded for it. I want it to be gain, and not loss; good, and not evil; success, and not failure; in order that I shall not regret the price that I have paid for it."

-    *Dr. Heartsill Wilson*

Victoria Jackson – Comedienne (*Saturday Night Live*)

Victoria Jackson's father was a gym coach, so it is not surprising that for the very first of the comedienne's twenty appearances on the *Tonight Show with Johnny Carson*, she would decide to recite poetry while executing a handstand!

Victoria is best known for her six years as a cast member on *Saturday Night Live*. Although she still performs, her main attention is devoted to her two children. Victoria also has created several children's albums in which she sings and plays the ukulele.

Victoria is married to her high school sweetheart. She is very upfront about her faith in Jesus. In her Web site biography, Victoria tells her fans to read and reflect on the following biblical passages:

- John 3:16
- Ephesians 2:8-9
- Romans 3:23
- Romans 6:23
- Entire book of John

Here is Victoria Jackson's prayer:

Dear Heavenly Father,

You are awesome, a brilliant Creator. Nature is so beautiful. That hummingbird and her little nest and babies was especially amazing. Thank you for letting me see that up close. Hallowed is your name. Thank you for your forgiveness to me. Help me forgive the people who are mean to me. (You know who they are.) Please bless my enemies and heal my six sick friends (T, R, J, C, L, and A) as soon as possible. They are in a hard spot right now. Please be right there with them and make it not so bad. Please protect our country and our world from terrorists. Please protect President Bush and give him your wisdom and your peace and joy. He has a tough job. Please forgive our country and let there be a revival. Let there be prayer and bibles in schools again. Let all the Christians, like me, live like it, stand up, and be strong. Thank you for my millions of blessings, especially my family. Please protect them with your angels. Please let my daughters marry the man you pick out for them. Please help me to know how to make my upcoming decisions. What is your will? Please give me work to do that is exciting and fulfilling and that brings glory to you. Can I have a little touch of your creativity? And for my friends who don't know you, please remove the blindfold from their eyes so they can see you, and Lord, I believe, help thou mine unbelief. I love you. In Jesus' name, Amen.

Dr. William N. Jackson – Pastor and famous preacher

I am writing this book at our cottage, which is situated on Chautauqua Lake in the little village of Ashville, New York. Just nine miles to our north is located the famous cultural vacation community, the Chautauqua Institution, which was founded in 1874. The world seems so much smaller when I read that Dr. Jackson was, for six years, the Director of the Department of Religion at the Institution.

Dr. Jackson is a Presbyterian minister who is the son of a Presbyterian minister. Reverend Jackson has been associated with parishes in Pennsylvania, Ohio, and Michigan. His life before the seminary included stints as a teacher and basketball coach.

Reverend Jackson is renowned for his work as a pastor and his special talent as a preacher. In fact, he is still called upon in the summer months to occasionally head the Sunday ecumenical worship services at the Chautauqua Institution.

Dr. Jackson sent us several beautiful prayers, two of which we are printing below:

> *Lord, when I am hungry, give me someone in need of food. When I am thirsty, send me someone in need of a drink. When I am cold, send me someone to warm. When I am grieved, offer me someone to console. When I am found in poverty, lead me to someone who is in a deeper need. When I feel as though I have no time, give me someone to whom I can give help, even for a little while. When I am humiliated, let me have someone I can praise. When I am disheartened, send me someone to cheer. When I need the understanding of people around me, give me someone who needs my understanding. When I want to be looked after, send me someone to care for. When I think only of myself, draw my thoughts and concerns to another. And when my cross grows heavy, let me share the cross of another. Amen.*

(Anonymous prayer of a Japanese Christian)

> *Come, Holy Spirit, come;*
> *Come as the fire and burn;*
> *Come as the wind and cleanse;*
> *Come as the light and reveal;*
> *Connect; convert; and consecrate,*
> *Until we are wholly (totally) thine.*

(Anonymous prayer from the Middle Ages)

Ann Jillian –
Actress

Ann's birth name was Ann Jura Nauseda. She is the daughter of Lithuanian war refugees. Because she has successfully battled breast cancer (1985), she has been an inspiration to more people than I'm sure she realizes. Ann's cancer episode has particular meaning for our family, as my wife Patrice has battled both breast and kidney cancer.

In my youth, one of my all-time favorite movies starred Laurel and Hardy, *Babes in Toyland*. In Ann Jillian's movie debut, she played "Bo Peep" in the 1961 remake of this film classic.

Jillian then played "Millie Ballard" on the TV sitcom *Hazel*. That series would be one of four sitcoms with which she was associated. The others included *It's a Living, Jennifer Slept Here*, and *Ann Jillian*.

After *Hazel*, Ann dedicated the next three years to studying psychology in college.

When Ann first returned to show business, she demonstrated her versatility as an entertainer by creating a singing duet with Debra Shulman. Ann went on to earn three Emmy nominations for her acting performances in *Mae West* (1982), *Ellis Island* (1985), and *The Ann Jillian Story* (1988).

Ann married Andy Murcia, a former police officer, who became her manager. The couple have a son, Andrew.

With her dark hair, I never realized it was Ann who played the role of the sexy neighbor in the movie *Mr. Mom*.

☆　　☆　　☆

Ann's husband, Andy, wrote that the Prayer of St. Francis De Sales was the prayer Ann first read on the day she learned she had breast cancer back in 1985. The prayer has become the favorite of both Ann and Andy, and they suggest it to anyone facing the battle with cancer.

> *The same*
> *everlasting Father*
> *who cares for you today*
> *will take care of you*
> *tomorrow and every day.*
> *Either He will shield you*
> *from suffering,*
> *or he will give you*
> *unfailing strength to bear it.*
> *Be at peace then*
> *and put aside*
> *all anxious thoughts*
> *and imaginings.*

Shirley Mae Jones – Actress (Movie/Broadway/TV)

Shirley Jones, the only child of Paul and Marjorie Jones, was named after Shirley Temple.

Shirley's vocal talent was recognized at an early age when she became the youngest member of her church choir at the age of six. In 1952, at the age of eighteen, Shirley won the Miss Pittsburgh beauty pageant and subsequently was runner-up in the Miss Pennsylvania contest. As a result of her placement in this competition, she was given a two-year scholarship to drama school.

Shirley's big break came after this apprenticeship. Ms. Jones won the role of Laurey Williams at an open-call audition for the motion picture adaptation of the musical *Oklahoma*.

Since that first motion picture, Shirley's career has been filled with any number of TV, movie, Broadway plays, and recording performances. In 1960, she was awarded an Oscar for best supporting actress for her role as Lulu Baines in *Elmer Gantry*. But for all her wide range of achievements, Shirley is probably best known today for her role as Shirley Partridge on *The Partridge Family*, which ran from 1970 to 1974. Her stepson, David Cassidy, would play the oldest of her Partridge children, Keith.

Jones had three sons and one stepson through her marriage to Jack Cassidy. The couple divorced in 1974, and Shirley has been married to Marty Ingels since 1977.

Shirley Jones was kind enough to send us a prayer from New York City, where she was performing in *42nd Street*:

> *"Thank you, Lord, for holding my hand every step of the way."*

Al Kaline –
Hall of Fame baseball player/Detroit Tigers

There aren't too many sports figures anymore who spend their entire careers with one team. It is understandable, then, that Al Kaline is beloved by Detroit Tigers fans for his loyalty as well as his superior play over a twenty-two year period (1954-1974) with their club.

Over his entire career with Detroit, Kaline amassed some impressive numbers that landed him in the Baseball Hall of Fame. During his 2,834 games, he collected 3,007 hits, which included 498 doubles, 75 triples, 399 home runs, 1,622 runs scored, and 1,583 runs batted in. Even though Al batted over .300 in eight different seasons, his only batting title came in 1955, in only his second season. At twenty-one years of age, he was the youngest person to ever have won this award.

Al was also known for his strong arm in the outfield and his fine defensive play. He led the American League in assists in both 1956 (eighteen) and in 1958 (twenty-three). It is hard to believe, but in 1971, he led the majors with a 1.000 fielding percentage!

Here is Al Kaline's favorite prayer:

> *"Dear God, I know that I am a sinner and in need*
> *of a savior. Thank you for sending your son Jesus*
> *to die for my sins, then raising Him to life. I turn*
> *from my sins and invite you to come into my life.*
> *Help me to live my life to praise you. In Jesus' name.*
> *Amen."*

Bil Keane –
Family Circus cartoonist

Bil Keane's cartoon, *The Family Circus,* is carried by 1,500 newspapers, making it the most widely syndicated comic strip in the world! Bil started *Family Circus* in 1960. The daily cartoon is in the shape of a circle to emphasize the closeness of the family unit.

Bil and his wife Thel (always the first reader of each comic creation) have five children and nine grandchildren. His real-life family is composed of Gayle, Neal, Glen, Christopher, and Jeff. His comic strip family includes Billy (modeled after Glen), Dolly (a pet name for Gayle), Jeffy (after Jeff), and PJ. Just like their real-life counterparts, the comic strip family had two dogs and a cat.

Three of the Keane kids today help with the family business. Jeff's name is now added to Bil's on the daily strip. Jeff now helps his father with the daily strip and is expected one day to assume full responsibility for the cartoon. Glen has gone on to become a direction animator for Disney Studios. The Disney characters that Glen has drawn include Ariel *(The Little Mermaid)*, Beast *(Beauty and the Beast)*, and the title characters in both *Pocahontas* and *Tarzan*.

Gayle takes care of much of the mail and the marketing requests.

The Keanes are good friends with the family of Erma Bombeck. The Keanes, Bombecks, and a few other neighbors would traditionally gather at the Keane house for a Christmas Eve mass.

Bil Keane accompanied his prayer with this note: "Dear Chuck: Here's my special prayer. Though not unique, it's been my favorite for many decades. I've said it in church, at the drawing board, while jogging, lying in bed, anywhere."

Memorare

Remember, O most gracious Virgin Mary, that anyone who fled to your protection, implored your help, or sought your intercession, was left unaided.
Inspired by this confidence, I fly to you, O virgin of virgins, my mother. To you I come before you I stand,
(kneel, sit, lie, swim, etc. whichever suits)
sinful and sorrowful.
O mother of the Word Incarnate! Despise not my petitions, but In your mercy hear and answer them. Amen.

Rex Kern –
Quarterback – The Ohio State University

In 1968, I came to Cleveland, Ohio, from Naperville, Illinois to start my teaching career. Being a sports fan, I was delighted that the Ohio State Buckeye football team greeted my arrival by going undefeated and winning the national championship. Their coach was Woody Hayes, and the team featured a stellar cast of athletes including Jack Tatum, Jim Otis, John Brockington, Larry Zelina, Mike Sensibaugh, Tim Anderson, and Jim Stillwagon. The team's quarterback was sophomore Rex Kern.

During Kern's three years as quarterback, the Buckeyes were 27-2 and incredibly, never lost in OSU's horseshoe stadium! During Rex's tenure, OSU won two Big Ten titles and participated in two Rose Bowls. Rex was named MVP of the 1969 Rose Bowl in which OSU defeated O.J. Simpson's USC Trojans. Kern ended up third in the Heisman Trophy voting in 1969.

After college, Rex spent four years playing defensive back for the Baltimore Colts. After disk problems forced his retirement, Kern returned to OSU to earn his Ph.D. in education. In 2001, Rex was involved in an automobile accident that prompted his sixth surgery on his spine.

Rex and his wife Nancy have two sons. Interestingly, Rex met Nancy when she was a Rose Bowl princess at the 1968 Rose Bowl.

Few people remember that Rex played on OSU's freshmen basketball team along with Jim Cleamons.

☆   ☆   ☆

I think that Rex Kern's response is appropriate enough to print in its entirety:

Dear Chuck,

Praise God for your desire to serve Him in this undertaking. While the majority of my prayer life is spontaneous conversation, I do have many scripture and devotional guides that lead me in my prayer life.

From the beginning of my faith journey with Christ I have always treasured Oswald Chambers' writings in My Utmost for His Highest. Enclosed is a copy of Chambers August 23 devotion, "Prayer Choice and Prayer Conflict" from Matthew 6:6. "But when you pray, go into your room and shut the door and pray to your Father who is in secret; and your Father who sees in secret will reward you."

Another great guide is Rick Warren's bestseller, The Purpose-Driven Life. I especially enjoy Rick's first chapter: "It All Starts With God." The first day begins with the Bible verse from Colossians 1:16: "For in Him all things were created, in heaven and on earth, visible and invisible, whether thrones or dominions or principalities or authorities—all things were created through Him and for Him." Warren challenges us in the Point to Ponder: "It's not about me." He concludes with his Question to Consider: "In spite of all the advertising around me, how can I remind myself that life is really about living for God, not myself?"

The above passages have brought me great comfort and encouragement in my personal prayer life. God's blessings on your book.

Yours in Christ,
Rex

August 23ʳᵈ

<u>*Prayer Choice and Prayer Conflict*</u>

When thou prayest, enter into thy closet, and … pray to thy Father which is in secret." Matthew 6:6

Jesus did not say—Dream about thy Father in secret, but pray to thy Father in secret. Prayer is an effort of will. After we have entered our secret place and have shut the door, the most difficult thing to do is to pray; we cannot get our minds into working order, and the first thing that conflicts is wandering thoughts. The great battle in private prayer is the overcoming of mental wool-gathering. We have to discipline our minds and concentrate on willful prayer.

We must have a selected place for prayer and when we get there the plague of flies begins—this must be done, and that. "Shut thy door." A secret silence means to shut the door deliberately on emotions and remember God. God is in secret and He sees us from the secret place; He does not see us as other people see us, or as we see ourselves. When we live in the secret place it becomes impossible for us to doubt God, we become more sure of Him than of anything else. Your Father, Jesus says, is in secret and nowhere else. Enter the secret place, and right in the centre of the common round you find God there all the time. Get into the habit of dealing with God about everything. Unless in the first waking moment of the day, you learn to fling the door wide back and let God in, you will work on a wrong level all day; but swing the door wide open and pray to your Father in secret, and every public thing will be stamped with the presence of God.

Nancy Lopez Knight – Hall of Fame women's golfer

Nancy Lopez received her first set of golf clubs at the age of eight and just twenty-two years later, she became the youngest woman ever inducted into the LPGA Hall of Fame.

Since there was no girls' golf team at her high school, Goddard High, she played on the boys' team and helped them win two state championships. Nancy left the University of Tulsa to pursue a career as a professional golfer. Tragically, her mother died of a heart attack before she could see her daughter ever win on the pro tour. Nancy finished second in her first three professional tournaments. In that first year, she won nine tournaments and earned Rookie of the Year honors.

During her illustrious career, Nancy was named Player of the Year three times. I believe that what Mia Hamm has done more recently for women's soccer, Nancy Lopez had done earlier for women's golf. While Arnie Palmer had his Arnie's Army, Nancy Lopez had her Nancy's Navy.

In 1982, Nancy married professional baseball player Ray Knight (kind of like Mia and Nomar). The Knights have three daughters.

☆   ☆   ☆

Here is the favorite prayer from Nancy Lopez Knight:

> *"Dear God, Thank you for everything today. Thank you for my family and our health. Please always touch my heart to make me a better Christian. I love you."*

Don Larsen –
Pitched World Series perfect game

Babe Ruth will always be known as one of the greatest sluggers to have ever played the game of baseball. However, he also held for many years the record for the most career strikeouts.

Sports fans are funny and have selective memories. Don Larsen had a career record of eighty-one wins and ninety-one losses. In 1954, he compiled a terrible 3-21 record for the Baltimore Orioles. He was traded to the Yankees, and in 1956, he went 11-5. That year, Don was selected to start the second game of the World Series for the Yanks. Don got shelled for four runs and lasted less than two innings.

But hardly anyone remembers that loss because of Larsen's pitching performance in the fifth game of the Series. Don Larsen needed only ninety-seven pitches in the only perfect game recorded in World Series history.

The last batter for the Giants was thirty-five-year-old Dale Mitchell, a lifetime .315 hitter who was pinch-hitting for pitcher Sal Maglie. Maglie had pitched a fine five-hitter, and the fact that the score was 2-0 probably helped Larsen concentrate harder and achieve his masterpiece.

In total, Don had a fourteen-year career, during which time he pitched for eight different teams.

We are proud to have prayers from both Don and from Gil McDougald. Gil played shortstop and in the second inning was alert enough to throw out Jackie Robinson on a grounder that had bounced off third baseman's Andy Carey's glove.

Don sent us his favorite prayer, the 23rd Psalm:

> *The Lord is my shepherd, I shall not want.*
> *He makes me lie down in green pastures;*
> *He leads me beside still waters;*
> *He restores my soul.*
> *He leads me in right paths for his name's sake.*

Even though I walk through the darkest valley,
I fear no evil; for you are with me;
Your rod and your staff - they comfort me.
You prepare a table before me in the presence of mine enemies;
You anoint my head with oil; my cup overflows.
Surely goodness and mercy shall follow me all the days of my life.
And I will dwell in the house of the Lord my whole life long.

Joan Leslie – Movie actress

I was fascinated with Joan Leslie's biography. Here is a person who certainly has lived her life to the fullest! At the age of three, she was performing with her two older sisters, Mary and Betty Brodel. After seeing their act, movie comedian Eddie Cantor recommended the girls to friends at MGM. Movie studios changed Joan's last name from Brodel to Leslie to avoid confusion with another star, Joan Blondell.

Ms. Leslie performed in some major motion pictures opposite the top stars of the time. If you check the dates, you'll notice that Joan was just eighteen years old after her fourth major film—in which she starred with Fred Astaire!

Year:	Movie:	Character:	Co-star(s):
1941	*High Sierra*	Velma Baughman	Humphrey Bogart
1941	*Sergeant York*	Gracie Williams	Gary Cooper

1942	*Yankee Doodle Dandy*	Mary Cohan	James Cagney
1943	*The Sky's the Limit*	Joan Manion	Fred Astaire
1944	*Hollywood Canteen*	Joan Leslie	Betty Davis, Joan Crawford, John Garfield, Robert Hutton, Betty Brodel
1945	*Too Young to Know*	Sally Sawyer	Robert Hutton
1945	*Rhapsody in Blue*	Julie Adams	Robert Alda
1947	*Repeat Performance*	Sheila Page	Louis Hayward

☆　　☆　　☆

The above is just a partial list of the films in which Joan appeared during her career. There are two items in Ms. Leslie's biography that had me especially captivated. Joan took a big sabbatical from acting starting in late 1950s in order to do humanitarian work, to work on dress designs, and most importantly, to raise her identical twin daughters, named Patrice and Ellen. My wife, Patrice, and my daughter-in-law, Ellen, also cut back on their own careers to raise their families.

After her children were raised, Joan returned to the stage and screen in a more limited capacity. In fact, she even made a cameo appearance in the 1989 remake of *Repeat Performance* called *Turn Back the Clock.* Few Hollywood stars have had careers that spanned the length of time achieved by Joan in her career. However, I personally feel that her major Hollywood accomplishment was the length of her successful marriage. Joan married Dr. William Caldwell on St. Patrick's Day in 1950. Dr. Caldwell died a month after the couple celebrated their fiftieth wedding anniversary in the year 2000.

☆　　☆　　☆

One of my very favorite songs is "Angels Among Us" by the group Alabama. One of my very favorite prayers, "Angel of God" is the one sent by Joan Leslie. With her prayer, Joan sent the following note: "My mother taught this little prayer to me when I was very young and I taught it to my daughters when they were little."

Angel of God, my guardian dear
To whom God's love commits me here,
Ever this day be at my side,
To light, to guard, to rule, and guide. Amen

Tom Lester –
Eb Dawson on *Green Acres*

Tom Lester feels he has lived a gifted life. He grew up on his grandfather's farm in Laurel, Mississippi, far from the lights of Hollywood. At the age of ten, he turned his life over to the belief in Jesus Christ. At that same time, he had a deep-seated feeling that he was destined to be an actor in California. His acquaintances felt that Tom's goal was unrealistic since he was too skinny, too tall (6'4"), and had a distinctly Southern accent.

Tom received a B.A. degree in chemistry and biology and taught science and biology for one year at a school in Purcell, Oklahoma. Still, Tom's dream of an acting career remained and he felt he would never be satisfied if he didn't give it a chance. Lester headed out to Hollywood. There, he became involved in a little theater group and providentially came to win the role of "Eb Dawson" on the TV show *Green Acres*. Tom has always maintained that true success comes in becoming everything that one's God-given talents have gifted you to become.

Tom Lester has spoken to many religious groups concerning his faith. He has appeared with the evangelist Billy Graham. Tom was selected as Mississippi's Wildlife Farmer of the Year for his management of his 250-acre timber farm in the town of Vossburg, Mississippi.

Tom Lester's favorite prayer is the "Our Father"(Matthew 6:9-13 & Luke 11:2-4):

> *9v. Our Father, who art in heaven,*
> *Hallowed be thy name.*
> *10v. Thy kingdom come, thy will be done,*
> *On earth as it is in heaven.*
> *11v. Give us this day our daily bread*
> *12v. And forgive us our trespasses*
> *13v. As we forgive those who trespass against us.*
> *And lead us not into temptation*
> *But deliver us from evil.*

For thine is the kingdom, and the power, and the glory, for ever.
Amen.

Evangeline Lilly –
One of the stars of TV show *Lost*

Seat 27H of Oceanic Flight 815—anyone who is a real devotee of the TV series *Lost* knows that this seat was occupied by Katherine "Kate" Austen in the fateful crash that left forty-eight survivors stranded on an ominous island. Kate is played in the series by the Canadian actress Evangeline Lilly. Before her acting career took off, Lilly spent time in a variety of jobs that included modeling, waitressing, completing oil changes on big rigs, and yes, ironically enough, even serving as a flight attendant.

From an early age, Evangeline's personality seemed to be characterized by both an adventuresome spirit and an empathy towards the needs of those less fortunate.

Lilly accepted a job as a model to help pay for her degree in international relations at the University of British Columbia. "Evey" is fluent in French, worked with a missionary group, and founded a world development and human rights committee while in college.

Each year, *Maxim* magazine compiles a list of the "Hot 100"— meaning the one hundred most beautiful women with careers on the rise. In 2005 Evangeline was listed as number two, right after Eva Longoria.

Evangeline sent this beautiful reflection as her favorite prayer:

If my soul has turned perversely to the dark,
If I have left some brother wounded by the way,
If I have preferred my aims to thine,
If I have been impatient and would not wait;
If I have marred the pattern drawn out for my life,
If I have caused tears to those I love,
If my heart has murmured against thy will,
O Lord, forgive me.
　　　　　- F.B. Meyer

Art Linkletter – Entertainer (*House Party*)

Art Linkletter (born Arthur Gordon Kelley) was given up for adoption as an infant and raised by Reverend Linkletter. From these less-than-idyllic beginnings, Linkletter went on to become a legend in radio and TV.

Art is known and loved by America's middle-agers and seniors for his popular shows *The House Party, People are Funny,* and *Kids Say the Darnedest Things.*

One of TV's true pioneers, Art has amassed countless awards over his many years in show business. He has received ten honorary doctoral degrees while earning two Emmy Awards and a Grammy. The award for which he is most proud, however, is "Grandfather of the Year." Linkletter has written twenty-three books, been appointed to a number of presidential commissions, and even was named ambassador to Australia.

I hadn't realized that Mr. Linkletter is equally adept in the business world as he is in the entertainment industry. He has served on numerous boards of directors and is chairman of Linkletter Enterprises, which is involved in a variety of overseas real estate and development projects.

Mr. Linkletter wrote that he does not have a favorite prayer. Instead, he said, "I prefer to speak to God in my own way, and on behalf of my friends and family, and for world peace, etc." I could only imagine that when God listens to Art's prayers, He is thinking, "Art, you say the darnedest things!"

Dick Locher –
Cartoonist ("Dick Tracy")

Sure, Dick Locher was a pilot and aircraft designer in the U.S. Air Force. Sure, he has worked for the *Chicago Tribune* since 1973.

Sure, he has drawn the cartoon *Dick Tracy* since 1983. Sure, he won the Pulitzer Prize in 1983. Sure, he has written several books including *Dick Locher Draws Fire, Vote for Me, The Daze of Whine and Neurosis,* and *Flying Can Be Fun.* Sure, he has won numerous awards for his journalistic talents which include drawing and scripting.

But what I'll remember most about Dick Locher are two facts: First, he was born in Dubuque, Iowa, where both of my brothers and one nephew went to school (Loras College). And, second, for several years, he was a member, along with my mother, Louise Spinner, in the choir of Sts. Peter and Paul Catholic Church in Naperville, Illinois.

The comic strip *Dick Tracy* was created by Chester Gould. Gould retired in 1977 and died in 1985. Gould was succeeded by writer Max Allan Collins and artist Rick Fletcher. When Fletcher died in 1983, Locher teamed with writer Michael Kilian to continue to produce the legendary adventures of this famous detective.

Dick Locher sent in two prayers that were favorites of his.

Dear God,
  Let me be as I want others to be,
  Let me dignify the quality of life,
  Let me assist those who are without.
  Let me give assistance and praise to those who attempt to better themselves.
  Let me give voice to those who have no voice.
  Let me give thanks for your wonderful gifts—and let me use them wisely.

Let me be better tomorrow than I was today.

Let me see clearly your needs for tomorrow as I have seen them yesterday,

Let me find the good of this day as I have isolated your good of yesterday,

Let me find those who need help tomorrow as they who have beckoned yesterday,

Ask me what is the most good I have done, and I must answer, "I haven't done it yet."

Trini Lopez – Singer/actor

A bit of parental discipline made all the difference in the life of Trinidad "Trini" Lopez III. Trini's parents were from Mexico but moved to Dallas, Texas right after their marriage. His parents were very poor but worked very hard to forge a better life for their six children, who were born in the U.S.

When Trini was eleven years old, his dad spanked him for hanging around with the wrong crowd. To temper his reprimand, his father bought Trini a $12 guitar. Because of his family's dire financial status, Trini had to drop out of high school to help out with the money he could make with his playing and singing.

Trini's first record producer, King Records out of Cincinnati, wanted Trini to change his last name to something more "Anglo." Trini refused.

Trini then became a friend of Buddy Holly and his back-up band, The Crickets. After Holly's tragic death in a plane crash, the Crickets asked Trini to be their lead singer. This arrangement never did materialize, but it did bring Trini to Hollywood, where he became popular as a solo artist. Then Trini was introduced to Frank Sinatra who signed Lopez to Sinatra's own record label. From that album, Trini's single, "If I Had a Hammer," became a hit in twenty-five countries. In time, Trini's numerous hits would include "Lemon Tree," "Kansas City," "America," and "La Bamba."

Sinatra was also responsible for introducing Trini to the film industry. Trini appeared in a number of TV and motion picture projects. One of my favorites will always be the classic *The Dirty Dozen*.

Trini has never forgotten his rough economic times during his childhood and has been involved in a variety of charitable causes.

Trini wrote, in his response letter, "I have a lot of special prayers that I love very much. The prayer I am sending you is one that I say every night before I go to sleep. This prayer is said by a Catholic priest at every mass."

> *Dear Lord, grant us peace in our day. Please protect us from all anxiety as we wait in joyful hope for the coming of our Savior, your Son, Jesus Christ, now and forever.*

Susie Luchsinger – Country/gospel singer

Susie's maiden name is McEntire. Susie is just one of the many outstanding members of this famous cowboy family. Her grandfather, John, was the steer roping world champion in 1934. Her father, Clark, held this same title three times (1957, '58, and '61). Susie's sister, Reba, is one of country/western music's top stars.

Susie was the youngest of the four McEntire children. Her oldest two siblings, Alice and Pake, still are involved in ranching. Susie graduated from Oklahoma in 1980 with a B.A. degree in personnel management. She married Paul Luchsinger the following year, and the couple now have two sons and a daughter.

Paul and Susie formed the Psalms Ministries program. Through this association, they have administered religious services in which they can give a combination of witness testimony and concerts. During this same time, Susie has been recognized twice (1995-96) as Christian Country Artist of the Year as well as a nominee for the GMA Dove Award for both Recorded Song of the Year and Female Vocalist of the Year.

Here is Susie's favorite prayer from the psalms of King David (Psalms 139:24)

"Search if there be any wicked way within me."

Johnny Lujack –
Heisman Trophy QB for Notre Dame

After college, I moved from Chicago to Cleveland, where I taught high school history for thirty-three years. As often as we could, my wife, our son, and I would travel along I-90 West to Chicago to visit my mother in our hometown of Naperville. We often broke up this trip by stopping at Notre Dame University in South Bend, Indiana. Because of these trips, the Fighting Irish are still our son's favorite sports team. So I was thrilled to receive a prayer for this book from 1947 Heisman Trophy winner and Notre Dame quarterback Johnny Lujack.

It was Johnny's childhood dream to one day play for Notre Dame. However, coming out of high school, no one would have predicted the success he would have playing collegiate ball. In his freshman year, Lujack was competing against five other candidates for the quarterback spot. Four of them had been All-State in high school, and the other had been All-New England! Johnny jokes that he made All-County and only later did the university discover that there was only one high school in the county!

The Notre Dame quarterback during Lujack's sophomore year, Angelo Bertelli, won the 1943 Heisman Trophy, but Johnny got the opportunity to step in for him when Bertelli left college to join the Marines.

Lujack was a very versatile athlete for the Irish. He played both offense and defense for the team and even did the punting. As quarterback, Johnny led the Irish to three national championships! However, he may be best known for his defensive exploits. After his own stint in the Navy, Lujack returned to school in 1946. During the game against top-ranked Army, Johnny made a game-saving, open-field tackle to preserve a scoreless tie and keep the Irish undefeated for the year.

Johnny Lujack is one of the few Notre Dame athletes to have ever earned four letters (football, basketball, baseball, and track) in one year.

After college, Lujack played four years for the Chicago Bears, before an injury cut short his career. In his rookie year, he played defensive back, intercepted eight passes, and was named to the All-Pro Defensive Team. The next year, Johnny was switched to quarterback where he set a record for throwing for 468 yards in one game. In 1950, he was again named All-Pro, this time on the offensive squad.

The College News Service has rated Johnny number sixty-one in its list of the top 100 Greatest Football Players of All Time.

Here is Johnny Lujack's favorite prayer:

> *God grant me the Serenity*
> *to accept the things I cannot change,*
> *Courage to change the things I can, and*
> *Wisdom to know the difference.*

Katherine MacGregor –
Harriet Olsen on *Little House on the Prairie*

The TV series *Little House on the Prairie* lasted ten years. During this time, a generation of Americans grew up enthralled by the weekly adventures of the pioneer family from the plains of Kansas who migrated and set up a homestead in Walnut Grove, Minnesota. The series was based on the *Little House* novels written by Laura Ingalls Wilder.

The two endearing characters on the show were the father, Charles Ingalls, played by Michael Landon, and Charles's second daughter, Laura, played by Melissa Gilbert. The character of Laura is actually the author living out the stories that she has written.

However, the series also had a great supporting cast that lent a huge interest to each week's dramatic episode. Several of these characters in the TV series never actually appeared in any of the original *Little House* novels. One of these fictitious yet prominent persons was Harriet Oleson, who was played by Katherine MacGregor. Harriet was the meddling and rude wife of the town's humble store keeper, Nels Oleson.

Although Katherine MacGregor had appearances in other TV shows, she will always be remembered for her role as Harriet. Katherine is a strict vegetarian, a non-smoker, and a disciple of an Eastern religion based on the teachings of the late Swami Vivekananda. Ms. MacGregor writes that Vivekananda started this religion when he attended the Parliament of Religions at the 1893 Chicago World's Fair.

Ms. MacGregor wrote this note to accompany her beautiful prayer, which was "composed by the wife of Rama, an incarnation of God, as considered by the Hindu Religion. He lived several thousand years before Christ. The more I repeat it, the deeper it goes. I became a Vedantist in 1971. My Guru named me SHOBHA—means 'Spiritual Beauty' Ah!!"

<u>A Vedic Prayer</u>
Whatever it was that made
The Earth its Base,
The World its life
The wind its Pillar
Arranged the Lotus and the Moon
And covered All the folds of sky,
with itself inside,
To that MYSTERY
Indifferent to Differences,
To It, I Pray.
- Om, Ramanatha

Melissa Manchester –
Singer/songwriter

Melissa Manchester is a singer-songwriter whose major hits include: "Midnight Blue," "Whenever I Call You Friend," "Don't Cry Out Loud," "You Should Hear How She Talks about You," "After All This Time," "It's the Light," "Easy," "So's My Old Man," "I Got Eyes," and "Come in from the Rain."

Melissa started writing poetry and singing commercial jingles when she was fifteen. She was discovered by Bette Midler and Barry Manilow, and became one of the original Harlettes (the back-up singers for Ms. Midler).

Manchester was the first singer to have two music themes ("Ice Castles" and "The Promise") nominated in the same year (1980) for an Academy Award. She earned a Grammy in 1982 for the best female vocal performance for her hit "You Should Hear How She Talks about You."

After a ten-year hiatus from writing and producing albums, during which time she raised two children, Melissa came out in 2004 with an album entitled *When I Look Down the Road*.

Melissa sent us her "favorite way to end our dinnertime" prayer:

"Thank you, God, for your faith in us."

Rose Marie –
Comedienne (*Dick Van Dyke Show*)

Some performers, such as Madonna and Cher, are known simply by their first names. But show business personality Rose Marie precedes them with this distinction. Rose Marie Mazetta has been in the entertainment industry since she was three years old in 1926. Amazingly, she was given her own national radio show by NBC when she was five!

Throughout the intervening years, Rose Marie established a fine career in comedy and song. Although she has a long and solid record performing in nightclubs, Broadway, and movies, she will best be remembered for her two stints on TV. Rose Marie received three Emmy nominations for her role as veteran comedy writer and man-hunter Sally Rogers on *The Dick Van Dyke Show*. While she appeared in any number of TV game shows, Rosie is best known for her fourteen years as a regular on *Hollywood Squares*.

In the 1980s, Rose Marie toured the U.S. with a revue called *4 Girls 4*. Her show business co-stars on the tour included Rosemary Clooney, Helen O'Connell, Margaret Whiting, and later, Kay Starr.

Rose Marie was married for nineteen years to Bobby Guy, first trumpeter in the NBC orchestra. Bobby died in 1964 and Rosie never remarried. The couple had one daughter named Georgiana.

☆　　☆　　☆

Rose Marie wrote a nice letter with her prayer. In the letter, she explained, "My favorite meditation is the 'Hail Mary.' I am a Catholic and have been saying this since I was old enough to do so. In addition, I am a great follower of the Virgin Mary and St. Jude." [Author's note: Before I print the Hail Mary, I should share with you that I have long ago, out of habit, substituted, "Pray for us Spinners" for "pray for us sinners"!]

The Hail Mary
Hail Mary, full of grace,
The Lord is with you.
Blessed art thou amongst women
And blessed is the fruit of thy womb, Jesus.
Holy Mary, Mother of God.
Pray for us Sinners
Now and at the hour of our death. Amen.

Jack Marschall – Cleveland News Anchor

The business of TV news broadcasting is a very transient one. News personalities move in and out of markets on a very regular basis. Despite this tendency, Cleveland has been blessed with a number of veteran news and weather persons whose names over the years have become very familiar to Clevelanders: Dick Goddard, Tim Taylor, Ted Henry, Denise Dufala, Wilma Scott, and Jack Marschall.

Jack Marschall graduated from Kent State University with a degree in journalism in 1975. After graduation, he began his career progressing through a number of Ohio markets (Zanesville '75-77, Youngstown '77-79, and Dayton '79-82) before settling in Cleveland.

The award-winning Marschall's popularity is attested to by the fact that he has been able to have a distinguished broadcasting career in Cleveland for nearly a quarter of a century, all the while raising his family in a stable environment and being integrally involved in his community.

September 11th, 2001, will always be remembered as the tragic day when terrorists hijacked four planes and flew three of them into the World Trade Center and the Pentagon. However, this month and day will have an additional significance for at least one special person. Jack Marschall is a living organ donor and on September 11th, 2007, he gave one of his kidneys to someone (unknown to Marschall) whose kidneys were failing. I feel that Marschall exemplifies the character and spirit of the celebrities in this book. They are the type of people Winston Churchill was referring to when he stated: "We make a living by what we get, but we make a life by what we give."

The following prayer, the Memorare, has proven a powerful and favorite prayer of Jack's over the past several years.

Remember, O most Gracious Virgin Mary,
that never was it known that anyone who

fled to thy protection,
implored thy help, and
sought thy intercession, was left unaided.
Inspired with this confidence, I fly unto thee,
O Virgin of Virgins, my Mother;
To thee I come, before thee I stand, sinful and sorrowful.
O Mother of the Word Incarnate!
despise not my petitions, but in thy mercy,
hear and answer me. Amen.

Coach Jack McKeon – Two-time MLB Coach of the Year

In 2003, Florida Marlins coach Jack McKeon was seventy-two years old, and the oldest person to manage a World Series championship team. Only the legendary Connie Mack has managed a major league baseball team at an older (88) age.

But Jack McKeon's managerial success is not based merely on age, but mostly on performance. McKeon is a four-time minor league manager of the year (1958, '61, '69, '70) while twice winning the award at the major league level (1999- Reds; 2003- Marlins). He became the first Marlin manager ever to win Coach of the Year honors. It was the fourth time McKeon had taken over managerial reins during the middle of the baseball season, and this fifth different managerial post overall (KC Royals, Oakland A's, San

Diego Padres, Cincinnati Reds, and Florida Marlins). His 2003 award made him the first manager ever to receive the award after being hired during the season.

For ten years (1980-90), Coach McKeon served as VP of baseball operations with the San Diego Padres. In this position, he earned the nickname Trader Jack, for his propensity for pulling the trigger on big multi-player deals.

A hand injury helped end Jack's nearly ten-year minor league playing career as a catcher. In 1951, when he was only twenty-one years of age, McKeon as a player/manager led his Sampson (NY) Air Force Base team to the Air Force championship.

Jack and his wife, Carol Isley, have two daughters and two sons. In high school, Jack was a starter on his New Jersey high school state championship squad.

Coach McKeon's favorite prayer is "My Novena Rose Prayer" of St. Therese, "the little flower."

O little Therese of the Child Jesus,
Please pick for me a rose from
The heavenly gardens and
Send it to me as a message of love.

O little Flower of Jesus,
Ask God today to grant the favors I
Now have place with confidence
In your hands.

(Mention Specific Requests)

St. Therese, help me to always
Believe as you did, in God's great
Love for me, so that I might
Imitate your "Little Way" each day.

Amen.

Gilbert "Gil" James McDougald – New York Yankee baseball player

Gil McDougald played his entire major league career with the New York Yankees. Reliable number 12 was awarded Rookie of the Year honors in 1951 and was the first rookie to hit a grand slam in a World Series.

McDougald was a very versatile player, and throughout his career, split his playing time between second, third, and shortstop positions. Gil was named to the American League All-Star squad five times ('52, '56, '57, '58, '59).

Gil is remembered by many baseball historians especially for two specific plays in his career—one defensive and one offensive. In the second inning of the fifth game of the 1956 World Series, Gil helped preserve Don Larsen's perfect game by alertly throwing out Jackie Robinson on a ground ball that had first bounced off the glove of third baseman Andy Carey.

And in 1957, he hit a line drive back to the mound that struck Cleveland's Herb Score in the eye. The blow seriously injured

Score and certainly curtailed a very promising career. Gil was tormented by his part in this tragic event, but was consoled by a long phone conversation he had with Score's mother. What people don't realize is that the incident that shortened Score's career most probably had an effect on McDougald's tenure as well. A career .289 hitter before the accident, Gil batted just .253 in his final three years. Though only thirty years old, he retired rather than report to the Washington Senators who had selected him in the expansion draft.

Gil McDougal sent me a pocket card with the Prayer of St. Francis printed on it. He said that it has been his favorite prayer and certainly hard to live up to.

Prayer of St. Francis

Lord,
make me an instrument of thy peace.
where there is hatred, let me sow love.
where there is injury, pardon.
where there is doubt, faith.
where there is despair, hope.
where there is darkness, light.
and where there is sadness, joy.

Divine Master
grant that I may not so much
seek to be consoled as to console.
to be understood as to understand.
to be loved as to love.

for it is in giving that we receive.
it is in pardoning that we are pardoned.
and it is in dying that we are born to eternal life.

Scott McGregor – Baltimore Oriole pitcher

Scott McGregor is the pitcher who turned preacher! Scott had an outstanding thirteen-year career with the Baltimore Orioles. In the midst of his career, in 1979, he turned his life to God. McGregor attended divinity school and eventually would become an ordained minister.

McGregor compiled an outstanding 51-4 record while at El Segundo High School in Southern California (one of his high school teammates was future Hall of Famer George Brett). Scott was drafted by the Yankees in the first round (fourteenth overall pick) of the 1972 draft. Before he reached the majors, the Yankees traded him to the Orioles in 1976 in a ten-player swap.

From 1976 until he was released in 1988, Scott put up impressive numbers. He pitched 2,140 innings, and had a 138-108 win-loss record, which included eighty-three complete games and twenty-three shutouts. His masterful control is illustrated by his 904-518 strikeout-to-walk ratio. He had a 1-1 record in both the 1979 World Series against the Pirates that the Orioles lost and also in the 1983 Series against the Phillies that Baltimore won. He lost the final game of the '79 Series, but pitched a complete game shutout in the 1983 championship game.

Scott and his wife Cara live in Towson, Maryland. Beside his pastoral duties, Scott is the pitching coach for the Orioles' farm system, most recently with the Bowie Bay Sox of the Eastern League.

In September of 2004, Scott was honored by being named one of the fifty all-time favorite Oriole players.

Scott picked as his favorite prayer, Psalm 51:

> *Have mercy on me, O God,*
> *according to your steadfast love;*
> *according to your abundant mercy*
> *blot out my transgressions.*
> *Wash me thoroughly from my iniquity,*
> *and cleanse me from my sin.*
>
> *For I know my transgressions,*
> *and my sin is ever before me.*
> *Against you, you alone, have I sinned,*
> *and done what is evil in your sight,*
> *so that you are justified in your sentence*
> *and blameless when you pass judgment.*
> *Indeed, I was born guilty,*
> *a sinner when my mother conceived me.*
>
> *You desire truth in the inward being;*
> *therefore teach me wisdom in my secret heart.*
> *Purge me with hyssop, and I shall be clean;*
> *wash me, and I shall be whiter than snow.*
> *Let me hear joy and gladness;*

let the bones that you have crushed rejoice.
Hide your face from my sins,
and blot out all my iniquities.

Create in me a clean heart, O God,
and put a new and right spirit within me.
Do not cast me away from your presence,
and do not take your holy spirit from me.
Restore to me the joy of your salvation,
and sustain in me a willing spirit.

Then I will teach transgressors your ways,
and sinners will return to you.
Deliver me from bloodshed, O God,
O God of my salvation,
and my tongue will sing aloud of your
deliverance.

O Lord, open my lips,
and my mouth will declare your praise.
For you have no delight in sacrifice;
if I were to give a burnt offering, you would
not be pleased.
There they shall be in great terror,
in terror such as has not been.
For God will scatter the bones of the ungodly;
they will be put to shame, for God has
rejected them.

O that deliverance for Israel would come from Zion!
when God restores the fortunes of his people,
Jacob will rejoice; Israel will be glad.

John McVay –
VP/GM of San Francisco 49ers

Throughout the world of sports, Miami (Ohio) University is recognized as "the Cradle of Coaches" for its history of developing future football coaching greats who, at one time, either played or started their coaching careers with the Red Hawks. Some of these luminaries include: Paul Brown, Woody Hayes, Bill Arnsparger, Weeb Ewbank, Sid Gillman, Ara Parseghian, Bo Schembechler, John Pont, Jim Tressel, Randy Walker, Ron Zook, Bill Mallory, Paul Dietzel, and John McVay.

John McVay extended this "Cradle of Coaches" reputation when he went from coaching to a very successful career as VP and general manager for the San Francisco '49ers.

McVay was a three-year letterman at the center position for Miami. He captained the squad his senior year while also earning All-Mid-American Conference honors. While in college, John was fortunate to be coached by both Woody Hayes and Ara Parseghian.

After graduation ('53), John compiled a 41-7-2 record as head coach at Canton Central Catholic. He added to his coaching credentials in his eight years as head coach of the Dayton Flyers. Coach McVay then led the Memphis Southmen of the World Football League to an impressive 24-8 record. John was handed the reins as New York Giants coach halfway through the 1976 season and held that position through 1978. McVay topped off his successful career in football with his final seventeen years as VP and general manager of the '49ers. During his tenure, the '49ers were in five Super Bowls, and he was rewarded for his efforts by being named NFL Executive of the Year in 1989. McVay retired in 1996.

☆ ☆ ☆

John McVay's favorite method of prayer is dialoging with God. He writes:

> *"Many of us are accustomed to reciting, from memory, certain prayers. I believe that the formal prayers we learned to recite as children are just a way to 'get us started' talking to God, and after saying the Lord's Prayer, we then begin talking to God in our own words—thanking him, asking for favors to become better husbands, fathers, brothers, etc. This dialogue, to me, is my favorite prayer."*

Patrice Munsel – Opera singer

Patrice Munsel is my wife's namesake, so my wife and I were both thrilled to get a prayer from her.

Ms. Munsel was born in Seattle and her last name was originally spelled Munsil. Her father was a dentist. Her mother saw the talent in her daughter at a very early age. Being very agile and athletic, Patrice played on the girls' football team at Lewis and Clark High School.

When Patrice was just sixteen, her mother took her to New York for preparation in vocal training, acting, opera singing, and language training in both French and Italian.

In 1943, Patrice won first place in a radio contest called the Metropolitan Auditions of the Air. Her prize was $1000 and a contract with the Met. As a result, by the time she was twenty-seven, Patrice had starred in more than twelve roles in the Met Opera. Ms. Munsel entertained the troops in World War II. She could sing both operatic and popular tunes, do ballet, tap dance, and even perform rhythmic whistling.

Beside her operatic career with the Met, Patrice starred in several movies and made guest appearances on the then-new medium of TV.

☆   ☆   ☆

Patrice Munsel sends this prayer as her favorite:

> *"Dear God,*
> *Please help me keep the joy in my life every day and help me bring Joy into the lives of my friends and loved ones."*

Queen Noor – Queen of Jordan

I think that when most of us think of a queen of a country, we think of a mainly ceremonial position. Well, you can throw all of those preconceived notions out the window when you consider the reign of Her Majesty, Queen Noor of Jordan.

Queen Noor's birth name is Lisa Najeeb Halaby. She was born to a very distinguished Arab-American family. Lisa became a member of Princeton University's first ever co-educational freshmen class. In 1974, she received a B.A. in architecture and urban planning.

Lisa became royalty through her marriage on June 15, 1978 to King Hussein of Jordan. Their majesties had two sons and two daughters. The royal family also has two children from King Hussein's previous marriage.

The impact that Queen Noor has made on her nation in the areas of children's welfare, health care, education, cultural enrichment, leadership encouragement, empowerment of women, enterprise development, historical appreciation, wildlife preservation, betterment of U.S.-Jordanian relations, and cross-cultural understanding among nations and peoples of the world is truly awe-inspiring. Queen Noor is also a determined advocate in the fight to ban antipersonnel mines and to eliminate world hunger.

Amid these many involvements, the queen finds time for her interests in snow skiing, water skiing, tennis, horseback riding, reading, gardening, and photography. She speaks Arabic, English, and French.

There are 117 prayer responses from celebrities in this book. People have asked me whom I would most like to meet from among all of these famous people. I'd have to say that Queen Noor would be very, very high on such a list.

Queen Noor's chief of staff, Nicole Carey, wrote on behalf of Her Majesty that the Queen was providing "a short quote from the Prophet Mohammed that Her Majesty uses in her speeches to relay the idea of the golden rule and the need to recognize our shared humanity":

> *The three great Monotheistic faiths, Judaism, Christianity, and Islam, spring from the same root, the faith of Abraham, and teach common values and principles which can and should be a unifying force among their believers—respect for freedom, justice, equity and compassion summed up in the commandment of our one God as stated by the Prophet, Mohammed PBUH: "None of you is a believer until he loves for his brother what he loves for himself" (Islam. Forty Hadith of an-Nawawi 13).*

> *Moderates of all creeds have a sacred duty to embrace these universal values, and begin to join forces to drown out those who cloak hatred in religious rhetoric. That is the route to genuine human security and to peace. We all need to make a leap of faith—faith in our shared humanity.*

John Jordan "Buck" O'Neil – Negro League baseball player

One of the finest gentlemen I've had the pleasure of meeting was ex-major leaguer David Pope. Dave played in the Negro Leagues, was brought up to the major leagues, and eventually played for the Cleveland Indians when they lost the 1954 World Series to the New York Giants. When he retired, Dave would come into my classes to give motivational talks to my students.

Dave Pope died several years ago, but I am fortunate to have received a prayer from another former representative of the Negro Leagues, Buck O'Neill. Buck played the majority of his Negro League career with the Kansas City Monarchs. His playing days were interrupted by a tour of duty with the U.S. Navy from 1944-45. Buck then toured with the 1946 Satchel Paige All-Stars before managing the Monarchs from 1948-55. Some of Buck's Monarch players who later played in the major leagues include Ernie Banks, George Altman, Elston Howard, and Satchel Paige.

Buck never played ball in the majors. However, when he became coach of the Chicago Cubs, he made history by becoming the first African American to coach in the big leagues. Then, as a scout for the Cubs, he was responsible for discovering future stars Lou Brock and Joe Carter.

Buck does not credit those two events as his most significant or happiest moments, however. The honor of happiest day of his life goes to Easter Sunday, 1943. Buck was playing in a game in Memphis, Tennessee and he hit for the cycle (single, double, triple, and home run in one game). Moreover, it was the same day that he was introduced to the lady to whom he would be married for the next fifty-one years of his life!

Buck sent me this response as an example of his dialogue with his maker:

Dear God, whether I get anything else today, I want to make sure that I spend time loving you and loving other people—because that's what life is all about. I don't want to waste this day. Why would you give me another day if I'm going to waste it?

Tom Osborne –
Nebraska football coach/U.S. Representative/AD

Tom Osborne, Dean Smith, John Wooden, Lou Holtz, Vince Dooley, Bobby Bowden, Jim Tressel, Jack McKeon, Steve Alford, Mike Hargrove, Gerry Faust, Yogi Berra, John McVay, and Sam Rutigliano are among the greatest coaches in the history of sport. I am honored to have each of their favorite prayers included in this book. I admire them greatly. I believe what sets these men apart is that their legacy will not be confined to the win-lose records in their sport. Coach Tom Osborne's record of dedication and service to his community is an example of this statement.

A fourth-generation Nebraskan, Osborne played three years in the NFL (San Francisco and Washington) before becoming an assistant to Cornhusker coach Bob Devaney. Despite his heavy coaching workload, Tom earned both his master's and doctoral degrees in educational psychology from the university! During this same time Coach Osborne also served in the Nebraska National Guard from 1960 to 1966.

Osborne took over as Nebraska head coach in 1973, and during his reign, his teams won 255 games, went to bowl games every year, averaged more than ten wins a season, and never won less than nine games in any one year. His teams won thirteen conference championships, were ranked in every weekly AP poll from the start of the 1980 season onward, and were recognized as national champions in 1994, 1995, and 1997. At the time of his retirement his 255-49-3 record was the best winning percentage among active NCAA Division I coaches.

After his twenty-five-year tenure as the head coach, Osborne served three terms (2001-2007) as U.S. representative from Nebraska's Third Congressional District. He then was upset in the Republican primary in his 2006 bid to secure the gubernatorial nomination.

Tom Osborne was named the interim Athletic Director at Nebraska in October of 2007.

Coach/Congressman Osborne and his wife Nancy have three children.

☆　　☆　　☆

Tom Osborne sent his favorite scripture passage, which is from 2nd Timothy 1:7:

> *"for God did not give us a spirit of, cowardice, but rather*
> *a spirit of power and of love and of self-discipline."*

Charles Osgood –
Commentator

I was a newspaper carrier when I was a young kid. For some reason, I remember one specific day on the route; I now know it to be sometime in March of 1958. I parked my bike and sat on the curb and read the story behind the huge headline "Leopold Paroled.*" I think being confronted each day with those bold headlines in the *Chicago News,* the *Chicago American,* and the *Aurora Beacon-News* fueled my eventual career as a history teacher. I was interested to see that Charles Osgood credits a similar experience as a paper boy for his later interest in news journalism.

Charles was actually born Charles Osgood Wood III. His father was a train conductor. It was his mother who encouraged the early interest Charles had shown in music and radio.

In 1954, Charles earned a degree in economics from Fordham University. While at Fordham, Osgood worked at the college's radio station. His student colleagues at the station included Alan Alda (actor), Jack Haley Jr. (film producer), and Vince Scully (veteran sports announcer).

During his tour of duty with the Army ('55-58), Osgood put his talents to use when, as a member of the Army band, he served as their announcer.

Charles is best known for his radio news commentaries called "The Osgood Files," which he has produced since 1971. From 1981-1987, he was the anchor for the *CBS Sunday Night News.* When Charles Kuralt retired in 1994, Osgood succeeded him as host of *CBS News Sunday Morning.*

Charles has won three Emmys and three Peabody Awards. He lived out a dream when he played the piano and five-string banjo with the Boston Pops Orchestra and then the New York Pops.

Charles and his wife Jean Crafton were married in 1973, and have five children. In 1985 the National Father's Day Committee named Osgood "Father of the Year".

*The court case of Leopold and Loeb captivated America in 1924. Richard Loeb, 18, and Nathan Leopold, 19, had high I.Q.s and were from very wealthy families. Intent on committing the perfect murder, they killed fourteen year old Bobby Franks. Ultimately, they were arrested and represented in court by the well known attorney, Clarence Darrow. With overwhelming evidence against his clients, Darrow had the boys plead "guilty" and then saved them from the death penalty. His twelve hour closing remarks left the judge in tears. Loeb was killed by another inmate in 1936. Leopold was paroled in 1958, migrated to Puerto Rico, and died in 1971.

Charles Osgood has chosen as his favorite prayer the Prayer of Saint Francis:

> *O Lord, make me an instrument of Thy Peace!*
> *Where there is hatred, let me sow love.*
> *Where there is injury, pardon.*
> *Where there is discord, harmony.*
> *Where there is doubt, hope.*
> *Where there is darkness, light.*
> *Where there is sorrow, joy.*
>
> *Oh, Divine Master,*
> *Grant that I may not so much seek*
> *to be consoled as to console;*

to be understood as to understand;
to be loved as to love;
for it is in giving that we receive;
it is in pardoning that we are pardoned;
and it is in dying that we are born to Eternal Life.

Andy Pafko –
Chicago Cubs Baseball player

Andy Pafko had a long (seventeen years) and very respectable professional baseball career from 1943 to 1959. He was a five-time All-Star and accumulated a lifetime .285 average along with 213 home runs. Some of his teammates called Pafko "Pruschka" and, because of his versatility others called him "Handy Andy."

Andy is associated with several unusual bits of baseball trivia:
- The *smallest* crowd in Wrigley Field history was on hand to witness Andy's first major league game on September 24, 1943. Because of a downpour, only 314 diehard fans saw this rookie go two for three with four RBI's.
- Then on May 30, 1945, before the *largest* single-day crowd in Cubs history (46, 965), Andy again had a stellar offensive

performance as he had five hits and clubbed a home run in each game of the doubleheader the Cubs split against the Pirates.

- Andy played for pennant-winning teams for all three teams he played for in his career: Cubs (1945); Dodgers (1952), and Braves (1957, 1958).

- In probably the most famous playoff game to determine a pennant in baseball history (October 3, 1951), New York Giant Bobby Thomson's home run sailed into the bleachers over left fielder Andy Pafko's head as "The Giants win the pennant!"

Andy Pafko actually sent us two prayers that are favorites of his, the Lord's Prayer and the Meal Prayer:

The Lord's Prayer
(Mt. 6:9-13; Luke 11:2-4)
Our Father, who art in Heaven, hallowed be thy name,
Thy kingdom come, Thy will be done,
on earth as it is in Heaven. Give us this day our daily bread
and forgive us our trespasses, as we forgive those who
trespass against us. And lead us not into temptation
but deliver us from evil.

For thine is the kingdom, and the power, and the glory, forever.
Amen

The Meal Prayer
Come Lord Jesus be our guest; and let these gifts to us be blessed.

Patti Page – Singer

Patti Page was born Clara Ann Fowler and was one of eleven children. She began her musical career in Tulsa, Oklahoma on a radio program sponsored by Page milk. On the show, she used her birth name, Fowler. But when another performer named "Patti Page" left, Clara took her place—and her name.

During her career, Patti recorded more than 100 albums and 160 singles. Eighty-four of these hits made *Billboard's* Top 40. She also earned three gold albums and fifteen gold singles.

Patti and her first husband, Charles O'Curran, adopted two children. Ms. Page married Jerry Filiciotto in 1990.

It is hard for me to pick which one of Patti's songs I think is most famous. Her most well-known hits include "The Tennessee Waltz," "Have a Little Faith and Love Will Come to You," "Confess," "With My Eyes Wide Open I'm Dreaming," "All My Love," "I Went to Your Wedding," "Doggie in the Window," "Alleghany Moon," "Old Cape Cod" and "Hush, Hush, Sweet Charlotte."

Patti sent me her favorite reflection, the Prayer of Jabez from 1 Chronicles 4:10:

> *Jabez called on the God of Israel, saying,*
> *"Oh, that you would bless me,*
> *And enlarge my border,*
> *And that your hand might be with me,*
> *And that you would keep me from hurt and harm!"*
> *And God granted what he asked.*

Walter William "Billy" Pierce – Chicago White Sox pitcher

I was twelve years old when the Chicago White Sox finally beat the Cleveland Indians and the New York Yankees and advanced to the World Series. I was just the right age to become an avid fan of our city's World Series representatives.

Billy Pierce was our number one pitcher for the "Go Sox", and throughout my life, I have Billy frozen in time and was under the impression that he spent his entire eighteen years for our city's ball team. In my research for this written portrait of Billy, I found several interesting tidbits:

- Billy never played a game in the minors before his big-league debut at the age of eighteen.

- Billy started his career by playing two years with the Tigers, then spent thirteen years in Chicago, and finished his career with three years with the Giants.
- Billy was in the World Series with all three teams he played for.

Pierce's career record should have long ago earned him a position in the Baseball Hall of Fame. He was a seven-time All-Star selection (he started three of these games); he won a total of 211 games; he recorded 193 complete games; and registered 38 shutouts. His number—19—was retired in 1987 by the White Sox.

At the time, the dreaded enemies of the White Sox were the New York Yankees. Pierce's contemporary on the Yanks was another lefty, Whitey Ford, a member of the Hall of Fame. Billy Pierce has 18 more wins, 62 more complete games, 7 more shutouts, and 408 more strikeouts in his career than does Ford. Let's put Billy in the Baseball Hall of Fame, where he certainly belongs.

Billy writes that The Lord's Prayer (Mt 6: 9-13; Luke 11: 2-4) "is always my standby.":

Our Father, who art in Heaven, hallowed be thy name.
Thy kingdom come, thy will be done, on earth as it is in Heaven.
Give us this day our daily bread and forgive us our trespasses
As we forgive those who trespass against us.
And lead us not into temptation but deliver us from evil.

For thine is the kingdom, and the power, and the glory, forever.
Amen

Just like when he was pitching in the majors, Billy does not rely on just one favorite pitch, or in this case, prayer. He also feels that the Serenity Prayer is very meaningful:

Grant me the serenity to:
Accept the things I cannot change;
The courage to change the things I can;
And the wisdom to know the difference.

A. James Quinn –
Auxiliary Bishop of Cleveland, Ohio

For almost thirteen years, in the late 1970s and '80s, I was a member of the St. John Bosco Choir in Parma Heights, Ohio. The first time my wife ever heard me sing at home, she joked that I belonged on the stage—and that the next one was leaving in ten minutes! Anyway, our choir sang at the 11 AM mass every Sunday. And every Sunday, the presider at this mass was the then-Monsignor Quinn, a visiting clergyman from the cathedral in Cleveland.

I was impressed by several traits of the monsignor's. Each time any second graders received their First Communion at the 11 am mass, Monsignor Quinn would recognize the youngsters and give a brief history of the communicant's patron saint associated with their name. I've never seen anyone with a more comprehensive knowledge of the history of the saints.

Monsignor was also known for his good sermons. In fact, he published a book of a selection of his homilies. The monsignor related to me that on occasion, he has gone to a parish for mass and has recognized the sermon as one from his book.

Monsignor Quinn always appreciated the efforts of our choir. He eventually was transferred from the chancery office to become a pastor at a parish. And then in 1983, Monsignor Quinn became auxiliary bishop and vicar general of the Cleveland Diocese. With each of these moves, we thought we would lose touch with him because of the pressure of his ever-increasing responsibilities. However, each year one of our choir members, Millie Stautihar, prepares a dinner for the bishop and a few of the other choir couples, and everyone enjoys the engaging conversation that is sure to ensue on these occasions.

The bishop is a true renaissance man. Besides being a great speaker; he is a certified pilot, he has his law degree and is a member of the Ohio Bar, he snow skis and ice skates, and loves to travel to the home of his ancestors, the "Emerald Isle."

Here is the prayer that was e-mailed from Bishop Quinn:

We give thanks, Lord, for all your gifts.
Thanks for laughter and fun,
smiles and hugs, the hands of friends
and the warmth of family

We give thanks for all graces
that draw us to you.
Inspire us now to be better, and
don't let us be discouraged,

Give us in our struggle and sputter
Our daily bread and a bit of butter;
Give us health and friends to make,
And a bit to spare for others' sake;

Help us to work well together
and to enjoy our labors, so that
in work and play
the light of your goodness
shines through us,
Bless us and those we love.

Amen.
-A. James Quinn

Mary Lou Retton –
Olympic gold medal gymnast

Mary Lou Retton will always have a special place in my heart. My first batch of prayer requests were sent out to over 300 celebrities. Mary Lou was the very first person to respond to my letter.

I also feel a connection with Mary Lou because she is from Fairmont, West Virginia. Fairmont is located less than twenty miles from Morgantown, home of my alma mater, West Virginia University. Mary Lou's older sister, gymnast Shari Retton Timko, was WVU's first woman's sports All American and is in WVU's Hall of Fame. Her brother Ron played baseball at WVU. And her father Ronnie captained WVU's 1959 basketball team (can we say Jerry West?) which lost to California in the NCAA championship game.

Mary Lou, of course, won the 1984 all-around Olympics gymnastics competition in Los Angeles with her famous, perfect-ten final event vault. At sixteen years of age, she became the first female athlete to be pictured on a Wheaties box.

Mary Lou has been a great role model and has been active in a number of business endorsements as well as involved in a variety of charitable causes.

She is happily married and living with her husband, Shannon Kelly, and their two daughters.

☆   ☆   ☆

Here is Mary Lou's favorite prayer:

> *God be in my head and in my understanding.*
> *God be in my eyes and in my looking.*
> *God be in my mouth and in my speaking.*
> *God be in my heart and in my thinking.*
> *God be at my end and my departing.*

Bobby Richardson –
New York Yankee baseball player

Bobby Richardson established for himself a very solid reputation as an outstanding second baseman for the New York

Yankees. During his career, which lasted from 1955 to 1966 (all with New York), he won five consecutive Gold Gloves ('61-65). He and shortstop Tony Kubek led the league in double plays four times.

Bobby's defensive skills helped the Yankees win seven pennants. But it was in the World Series that his offensive skills rose to the surface. Although he was a career .266 hitter, in thirty-six World Series games, Richardson batted .305. Bobby was named the MVP of the 1960 World Series, even though the Yankees were defeated in that series by Bill Mazeroski and the Pittsburgh Pirates. He still remains as the only World Series MVP selected from the losing team. During that series, Bobby batted .367 with eleven hits, including a grand slam, eight runs scored, and twelve RBI's. (He had driven in only twenty-six runs during the entire regular season!)

In the 1961 Series, he batted .391, and in 1962, Richardson will always be remembered for snagging Willie McCovey's hard line drive with two on and two outs to end the game and win the Series for the Yankees.

After he retired from baseball, Bobby coached at the college level.

Bobby Richardson has always been known as an upright, principled human being.

Bobby Richardson's favorite prayer:

Father,
My prayer is not my will—but your will.
In Jesus' name.

Daniel "Rudy" Ruettiger –
Notre Dame football walk-on; *Rudy*

Andy Warhol claimed that everyone is entitled to fifteen minutes of fame in their lifetime. Daniel Ruettiger settled for only twenty-seven seconds of fame. But Daniel Ruettiger, better known as Rudy Ruettiger—better known as "Rudy"—has parlayed that half-minute of fame into a lifetime of focusing people's attention on what is possible to achieve in their lifetime.

Rudy's short stretch in the spotlight took place the afternoon of November 8, 1975. His dream had always been to play football for Notre Dame University. However, since he didn't have the grades to be accepted at Notre Dame, he first enrolled across the street at the two-year Holy Cross College (since 2003, Holy Cross now has a four-year baccalaureate program). Rudy persevered, and after two years, he was accepted to Notre Dame.

Rudy, all 5'6" and 165 pounds of him, talked himself onto the Irish practice squad. On the very last game of his senior year, Rudy was allowed to suit up (#45) for the game. He was inserted into the game for the last twenty-seven seconds, and made the last tackle of the game against the Georgia Tech quarterback. For his perseverance, Rudy became the only Irish player to have ever been carried off the field on the shoulders of his teammates.

After graduation, Rudy tried for sixteen years to market his story to film producers. Finally, in 1993, the same film team that created the 1986 classic, *Hoosiers*, came out with the film *Rudy*.

Daniel Ruettiger was the third of fourteen children and went to high school in Joliet, Illinois, just twenty-two miles from my own hometown of Naperville, Illinois. Rudy is now married, and he and his wife have two children.

Just a note—The next time you watch *Rudy*, you might want to watch for two things:

1. The band playing before Rudy's big game against Georgia Tech is actually the Penn State Blue Band.
2. Rudy actually makes an appearance in his own film. He is seated in the Irish cheering section behind actor Ned Beatty, who plays Rudy's father. Beatty tugs on Rudy's shirt during one of the exciting moments in the game.

Rudy's favorite prayer is surprisingly the one to Our Father, rather than the Hail Mary, or the prayer to "Our Lady", which translates to "Notre Dame."

The Our Father *(Matthew 6:9-13)*
9v. Our Father, who art in Heaven,
Hallowed be thy name.
10v. Thy kingdom come, they will be done,
On earth as it is in Heaven.
11v. Give us this day our daily bread
12v. And forgive us our trespasses
13v. As we forgive those who trespass against us.
And lead us not into temptation,
But deliver us from evil.

For thine is the kingdom, and the power, and the glory, forever. Amen.

Sam Rutigliano –
Coach: Browns, Liberty University, NFL Euro

My friend, Doug Dieken, was gracious enough to write the Foreword for this book of prayers. Doug was a member of the Cleveland Browns' "Kardiac Kids" teams of the early 1980s. His coach was Sam Rutigliano. "Riverboat Sam" provided Cleveland fans with an exciting brand of football. In 1981, Rutigliano's Browns came one play short of reaching the Super Bowl. In 1980, Sam was named NFL's Coach of the Year.

When I think of Coach Sam, I think of the phrase "grace under pressure." And appropriately enough, the book he authored is called *Pressure*. He and his wife Barbara have a lot to teach us about dealing with pressure. In 2004, the couple celebrated their fiftieth anniversary. However, like most marriages, their years were filled with tragedy as well as triumph. In 1962, the Rutiglianos faced the ultimate test to their marriage when their four-and-a-half-year-old daughter, Nancy, died in a car accident. It was—and is—their faith in God and the knowledge that they will one day be reunited with

Nancy that has allowed them to go on. Sam and Barbara's faith in God also has kept them centered when the Browns released Sam during the 1984 season.

After his time with the Browns, Sam spent the next eleven years as head coach of a Christian institution, Liberty University in Lynchburg, Virginia. Sam then spent five years as a TV football analyst before returning to the coaching ranks for NFL Europe. He has served coaching stints on staffs of the Barcelona Dragons, the Glasgow Tigers, and the Hamburg Sea Devils.

It is interesting to note that Coach Sam grew up in Sheepshead, New York, which is also the home of two of America's greatest football coaching legends, Vince Lombardi and Joe Paterno.

Coach Sam wrote:

"Chuck, in 1962, Barbara and I lost our four-and-a-half-year-old daughter. It was devastating. What do you do? Jesus Christ was the answer. Hebrews 11:1. *'Faith is the assurance of things hoped for and the certainty of things you cannot see.'* You believe without seeing!

In 1984, Fired by the Browns. God has a plan. It was the best thing that ever happened to me and my family!"

Ephesians 3:20: *Glory belongs to God whose power is at work in us. By this power he can do infinitely more than we can ask or imagine. Glory belongs to God in the church and in Christ Jesus for all time and eternity. Amen.*

Tim Salmon –
Anaheim Angels baseball player

Tim is one of the many celebrities in this book who not only have been outstanding in a particular field of endeavor, but who also have extended their resources to make a positive impact on the community.

Tim's parents divorced when he was young. He found consolation from the advice of his grandmother, who told him that whenever he would experience rough times, he could depend on his Heavenly Father to watch over him.

The only college to show a real interest in Tim's baseball ability was Grand Canyon College, a small school in Phoenix, Arizona. At the time, Tim didn't know or care that the school was a Christian college—he just wanted a chance to play ball. However, in 1987, he made the commitment to place his trust in Jesus.

In 1988, he helped Grand Canyon take second place in the NAIA World Series. He finished his collegiate career, setting school career records for most runs (225), home runs (51), and RBIs (192) while also setting a season record for walks (81).

In 1989, Salmon was selected in the third round of the free-agent draft by the California Angels. He was named Minor League Player of the Year in 1992, and was called up by the parent club in August of that same year. Tim's been in the majors and with the Angels ever since.

Tim has had a long and productive career with the Angels and was thrilled to be a major contributor for the 2002 team that beat the Giants in the World Series.

As I said in the beginning of this celebrity summary, Salmon has used his success and acclaim in the baseball world to support and sponsor a variety of charitable causes. In fact, Tim was recognized for his efforts by being named the team's nominee for the Roberto Clemente Man of the Year Award in 1998, 2002, and 2004. The award recognizes the baseball player who best exhibits sportsmanship, community involvement, and the individual contributions to his team. After a less-than-average year for Tim in 2001, he bounced back and won *The Sporting News'* 2002 Comeback Player of the Year Award. That same year, he was also awarded the Hutch Award, given to the player who shows "honor, courage, and dedication to baseball while overcoming adversity in their personal or professional lives."

Mike Salmon, Tim's brother, played safety for the San Francisco '49ers football team.

Tim and his wife, Marci, have four children.

On the back of the signed, printed card Tim sent me is a biblical passage that beautifully sums up Tim's emphasis on perseverance as a test of faith during our trials in life:

Consider it pure joy, my brothers, whenever you face trials of many kinds, because you know that the testing of your faith develops perseverance. Perseverance must finish its work so that you may be mature and complete, not lacking anything."
James 1:2-3

Joan Benoit Samuelson – Olympic gold medalist/marathon

Cape Elizabeth, Maine is not only the birthplace of movie director John Ford, the inspiration for Edward Hopper's painting, *Lighthouse Hall,* it is also the birthplace of Joan Benoit Samuelson, the winner of the first women's Olympic marathon.

When she was in high school, Joan Benoit broke her leg snow skiing. Her lifelong interest in running arose during the subsequent running that was part of her recovery therapy.

Joan entered her first Boston Marathon when she was a senior at Bowdoin College. Even though it was only her second marathon, she won in the American record time of 2:35:15.

In 1981, Benoit had surgery on both Achilles tendons. By 1983, she had returned to form and again won the Boston race, this time in the world record time of 2:22:43.

In 1984, Joan took first place in the U.S. Olympic trials, even though she had arthroscopic knee surgery just seventeen days before the race. The 1984 Los Angeles games included the first-ever Olympic marathon for women. Fifty runners from twenty-eight countries ran in this historic race. The odds-on favorite in the race was Norway's Grete Waitz—who had never lost a marathon that she had finished. Grete had previously beaten Joan in ten of eleven races.

However, the key to Joan's victory was her quick separation from the main pack after only about fourteen minutes into the race. Benoit ended up winning by a margin of one minute and twenty-six seconds over Waitz.

A month after the 1984 competition, Joan married her college boyfriend. The Samuelsons have two children.

Through the years, Joan has given of her time and energy to any number of charitable causes, and in 1998, established a world-class road race called Beaches to Beacon in her hometown.

☆   ☆   ☆

Joan's simple words gave me encouragement when I needed it. She said to *"Live your dreams and follow your heart."* She said that the following simple verse from the Bible motivated her in the 1984 Olympic marathon:

"First shall come last and last shall come first."

Cael Sanderson –
Four-time NCAA wrestling champ

I believe that Cael Sanderson is America's best-kept sports secret. Even some of my friends who are sports fanatics could not identify his name with his achievements.

Cael Sanderson is merely the only undefeated four-time wrestling champion in NCAA history. He is also the only person to be named Outstanding Wrestler at the NCAA wrestling championships all four years of his college career. He was also the first multiple winner of the Dan Hodge Award (which he won three times!) which is given annually to the nation's top collegiate wrestler. Only four of his forty collegiate matches his senior year at Iowa State lasted the full seven minutes. He also won a gold medal in Wrestling at the 2004 Athens Summer Olympics. He also has been featured on the front of the Wheaties cereal box. And in the April 1, 2002 edition of *Sports Illustrated,* his 159-0 collegiate wrestling record was ranked as the all-time number-two most outstanding individual achievement in the history of college athletics! Cael is also an outstanding artist who earned a degree in art and design from Iowa State University.

So how come more people don't know Cael Sanderson? Probably because he is a humble, centered man who is more interested in promoting God than himself. He comes from a wrestling family. His brothers Cody, Cole, and Cyler all are excellent wrestlers, and his father Steve was the boys' high school coach.

Cael and his wife Kelly have one child.

Oh, by the way, I know you would want to know what *Sports Illustrated* ranked as the number-one all-time greatest individual achievement in the history of collegiate athletics: On May 25, 1935, Jesse Owens, running for Ohio State, broke four world records in forty-five minutes at the annual Big Ten Track and Field Championships!

Cael Sanderson sent us two of his favorite scripture passages from the Book of Mormon:

Alma 34:38:
That ye contend no more
against the Holy Ghost, but that
ye receive it
and take upon you the name
of Christ; that ye humble
yourselves
even to the dust, and worship
God, in whatsoever place ye
may be in,
in spirit and in truth; and that
ye live in thanksgiving daily, for
the
many mercies and blessings
which he doth bestow upon you.

3 Nephi 13:19-20:
19. Lay not up for yourselves
treasures upon earth, where
moth and
rust doth corrupt, and thieves
break through and steal;
20. But lay up for yourselves
treasures in heaven, where
neither moth
nor rust doth corrupt, and
where thieves do not break
through nor steal.

Stephen Schwartz – Broadway producer

I'd guess it was in the early '80s when Normandy High School (Parma, Ohio) presented Stephen Schwartz's play *Pippin*. The school's drama coach, Wayne Moreland, asked around to see if any faculty members would be interested in having one of their kids audition for the part of Theo. Our son Scott got the role and subsequently had a great experience with a wonderfully talented high school director and cast. Now, twenty-some years later, I am thrilled to receive a prayer from the originator of the play that is associated with such fond family memories.

While he was still in high school, Stephen Schwartz studied piano and composition at the Julliard School of Music. He then went on to graduate from Carnegie Mellon University in 1968 with a B.F.A. in drama. Stephen is a tremendous talent and has won three Academy Awards, three Grammies, and three Drama Desk Awards, while also receiving five Tony nominations.

Some of Stephen's best known creations include: *Godspell, Pippin, The Magic Show, Children of Eden,* and *Wicked.* He also was responsible for writing the English texts for Leonard Bernstein's Mass, which was produced for the opening of the Kennedy Center for the Performing Arts.

Schwartz has also written a children's book, *The Perfect Peach* (1977). In addition, Stephen was the lyricist for the films *Pocahontas* (1995), *The Hunchback of Notre Dame* (1996), and *The Prince of Egypt* (1998).

The prayer that Stephen Schwartz sent is the lyrics from "In the Beginning," the finale of *Children of Eden*:

IN THE BEGINNING:

This step is once again our first
We set our feet upon a virgin land
We hold the promise of the Earth
In our hands
No flood from Heaven comes again
No deluge will destroy and purify
We hold the fate of man and men
In our hands
Now at this dawn so green and glad
We pray that we may long remember
How lovely was the world we had
In the beginning

Of all the gifts we have received
One is the most precious and most terrible
The will in each of us is free
It's in our hands
And if some day we hear a voice
If he should speak again
Our silent Father
All he will tell us is the choice

Is in our hands
Our hands can choose to drop the knife
Our hearts can choose to stop the hating
For ev'ry moment of our life
Is the beginning

There is no journey gone so far
So far we cannot stop and change direction
No doom is written in the stars
It's in our hands
It's in our hands
It's in our hands
We cannot know what will occur
Just make our journey worth the taking
And pray we're wiser than we were
In the beginning
It's the beginning
Now we begin

General H. Norman Schwarzkopf – General/Operation Desert Storm

Norman Schwarzkopf's father graduated from West Point, served in both World Wars, and rose to the rank of brigadier general. After World War II, the Schwarzkopf family lived in

Iran, then Switzerland, then Germany, and finally in Italy. The transient military life enabled Norman to become fluent in both French and German.

Upon his family's return to the States, Norman also attended West Point, where he made full use of his college years. He played football and wrestled, while also singing, and eventually conducting the chapel choir.

During his military career, Schwarzkopf led forces in the Vietnam War and Grenada, and taught engineering at the Point. He moved up the ranks and became a full four-star general in 1988. General Schwarzkopf is best known for leading the military forces during Operation Desert Shield as well as Operation Desert Storm. Through the six-week operation, U.S. forces liberated Kuwait and came within 150 miles of Baghdad before Iraq accepted a cease fire. U.S. casualties totaled 115 killed and 330 wounded.

Among the decorations the general has received are five Distinguished Service Medals, three Silver Stars, the Bronze Star, the Purple Heart, the Presidential Medal of Freedom, and the National Order of the Legion of Honor, as well as commendations from a number of countries throughout the world.

General Schwarzkopf has been married to his wife, Brenda Holsinger, since 1968. They have three children. Schwarzkopf retired from the military in 1992, the same year that he wrote his autobiography, *It Doesn't Take a Hero*.

General Schwarzkopf sent "one of the prayers that I said every night during the Gulf War."

"Dear Lord, please protect my family and protect my troops.
Thy will, not mine."

Paul Scofield –
Oscar winner/*A Man for all Seasons*

Paul Scofield is one of the most accomplished Shakespearian actors of our time. After his early training as an actor (he has been a professional actor since age fourteen), Paul toured with companies that entertained the British troops during World War II.

In 1955, Scofield was invited to play the role of Hamlet in the Soviet Union—the first English actor to be so invited for such a performance since the Russian Revolution of 1917. Paul has played most of the great Shakespearean parts, and has appeared in more than eighty plays in his spectacular career.

In the United States, he is perhaps best known for his more abbreviated but still illustrious film career. In 1966, he won an Academy Award for best actor for his performance as Sir Thomas More in *A Man for All Seasons*. He would wait twenty-eight more years until he was again nominated for another Oscar, this time for best supporting actor for his role as Mark Van Doren in the Robert Redford-directed movie, *Quiz Show*.

Scofield has held the position as both co-director for the Royal Shakespeare Company (1966-68) and as director of the National Theater (1971). A humble man, Scofield did something I would imagine few others have done: He turned down an offer for knighthood from Queen Elizabeth.

☆ ☆ ☆

Paul Scofield wrote in his response to our prayer request: "I have a book of the prayers of St. Thomas More and have been for many years a reader of them. I enclose a short passage which particularly appeals to me."

> *"Take from me, good Lord, this luke-warm fashion, or rather key-cold manner of meditation and this dullness in praying unto thee. And give me warmth, delight and quickness in thinking upon thee."*

Herb Score – Cleveland Indians pitcher/announcer

Two accidents had a great impact on Herb Score's life and could have been the defining characteristics of his résumé. But most fans in Cleveland will always remember their beloved Herb Score more for his potential as a dominating southpaw pitcher and for his performance during his thirty-four-year career as an announcer for the Indians.

Score won Rookie of the Year honors in 1955 by winning sixteen games. By also fanning 245 batters, he broke Grover Cleveland Alexander's long-standing rookie record. Herb's rookie strikeout record wouldn't be broken until 1984 by Dwight Gooden.

In just his second season, Score became a twenty-game winner, limited opposition batters to a .186 average, and recorded a league-leading five shutouts.

Then on May 7, 1957, Score's road to becoming a perennial all-star ball player would take a permanent detour. On that night, a screeching line drive back to the mound by Yankee Gil McDougal struck Score in the eye. Herb was out for the season, and when he attempted to resume his career the following year, he was never quite the same. Score pitched for the Indians in 1958 and 1959, and then for the White Sox, until he retired in 1962.

Although this tragic event must have been personally devastating, the same determination Score used as a great athlete enabled him to make a smooth transition into a very successful thirty-four-year career (four on TV and thirty on radio) as the voice of the Cleveland Indians.

Just a year after Score retired from broadcasting, on October 8, 1998, he was involved in a second tragic accident, which again seriously threatened his physical well-being. The car Score was driving collided with a tractor-trailer, and Herb suffered debilitating hip and head injuries.

The measure of how Herb Score is dealing with his second major physical setback can be seen in the fact that he painstakingly hand wrote the prayer that he graciously sent to me. Sportswriter Terry Pluto wrote that Rocky Colavito may have been the heart of Cleveland baseball, but Score has been its soul.

Due to his physical setbacks, it is difficult for Herb to put pen to paper. Still, his favorite prayer that he sent to me was handwritten.

Prayer to Saint Jude

"St. Jude Thaddeus, the name of the traitor who delivered your beloved Master into the hands of his enemies has caused you to be forgotten by many. But, the Church honors and respects you as the patron of hopeless causes. I invoke you to ask God to grant me this wish [mention here]. I will never cease to honor you and declare my power to encourage devotion to you. Amen."

George Beverly Shea –
Tenor/singer with Billy Graham Crusade

In the year 2001, *Today's Christian* magazine asked its readers to vote for their top worship songs of all time. (I will print the resulting Top 10 list at the end of this introduction.) The song that ranked at number two, right after "Amazing Grace," was "How Great Thou Art." The nine verses of this song were written by the Swedish pastor Carl Boberg. In 1948, Reverend Stuart K. Hine translated three stanzas into English and added an original fourth verse.

"How Great Thou Art" became popular in the United States when it was sung at Billy Graham Crusades by George Beverly Shea. Shea is the son of a Wesleyan Methodist minister, and he became known for his association with the Graham crusades that he joined in 1947. George has written a number of classic religious hymns, including, "The Wonder of It All," "Praise Him in the Morning," and "I'd Rather Have Jesus."

Through the years, Shea has been nominated for ten Grammys, and he won that award in 1965 for his album "Southland Favorites" with the Anita Kerr Singers. In 1965, he was honored by being elected into the Nashville Gospel Music Association's Hall of Fame.

George and his wife Karlene have two children.

Top Ten Worship Songs of All Time (*Today's Christian* magazine, Sept/Oct 2001):

1. "Amazing Grace"
2. "How Great Thou Art"
3. "Because He Lives"
4. "Great Is Thy Faithfulness"
5. "The Old Rugged Cross"
6. "What a Friend We Have in Jesus"
7. "To God Be the Glory"
8. "Majesty"
9. "Shout to the Lord"
10. "Holy, Holy, Holy"

George wrote: "In the Holy Bible we see, seemingly in glorious color, a word picture of God's wonderful provision of forgiveness and redemption, available to the believing heart." His favorite biblical passage is appropriately enough, Psalms 28:7:

> *The Lord is my strength and my shield; in him my heart trusts; so I am helped, and my heart exults, and with my song I give thanks to him.*

Martin Sheen – Actor/activist

Martin Sheen was born Ramon Gerardo Antonio Estevez. He was the seventh of ten children born to a Spanish father and an Irish mother who met at citizenship school in Dayton, Ohio. He took his stage name to honor theologian bishop, Fulton J. Sheen.

Martin's parents wanted him to attend the University of Dayton, but Sheen took a flyer (pun intended) on that goal in order to travel to New York and become an actor. After starring in the 1964 production of *The Subject was Roses* he left New York for Hollywood.

Sheen has compiled a remarkable resume of work on TV and on the large screen. His efforts have resulted in numerous awards and it came as no surprise when he was given a star on the Hollywood Walk of Fame.

Martin's most notable TV performances include: *That Certain Summer* (1972), *The Execution of Private Slovik* (1974), *The Missiles of October* (1974), *Kennedy* (1983), *Gettysburg* (1993), and *West Wing* (1999-2006).

On the big screen Sheen's two most memorable roles were in *Badlands* (1974) and *Apocalypse Now* (1979). He also had roles in the classic films: *The Final Countdown* (1980), *Wall Street* (1987), *Cadence* (1991), *Gandhi* (1982), and *The American President* (1995).

I am doing an injustice by highlighting just a few of the very many TV and film roles in which this great actor has been involved.

My dad died of a heart attack at the age of 50. Now that I'm over 60, I consider every day to be a gift. I'm sure that Martin feels that same way. At the age of 39, he personally survived a heart attack during the filming of *Apocalypse Now* in the Philippines.

Although Martin Sheen will long be remembered for his TV and film credits, I believe that his more important legacy will be his advocacy of liberal political causes. He has "walked the walk" as well as "talking the talk." He has been arrested over 70 times for protesting civil rights and governmental abuses. My favorite quote from Martin Sheen is that: "I love my country enough to suffer its wrath."

Martin is one of a good number of celebrities in this book of prayers who have been married to the same partner for a long period of time. He and his artist wife, Janet, were married in 1961 and have four children, all of whom are actors: Charlie Sheen, Emilio Estevez, Renee Estevez, and Ramon Estevez.

Martin's prayer is short and to the point:
"Jesus, mercy!"

Senator Alan K. Simpson –
U.S. Senator from Wyoming

In the year 430 BC, Pericles stated, "Just because you do not take an interest in politics, doesn't mean politics won't take an interest in you." In 1997, Senator Alan Simpson restated the same sentiment, "Take part or get taken apart."

Senator Simpson is from Cody, Wyoming, a town founded by William Frederick "Buffalo Bill" Cody himself. If the town has a great history, so does the Simpson family. Alan's great-great-grandfather first came to Wyoming as a member of the Conner expedition of 1862 and was at the Battle of the Fetterman Massacre. Alan's grandfather was a lawyer and so was his father. Alan's father was governor of Wyoming from 1954 to 1958 and U.S. senator from 1962 to 1966.

Alan earned his law degree from Wyoming University in 1958 and had a practice in Cody for the next eighteen years. He was voted into the state house of representatives in 1964 and served there for thirteen years. He then was elected and served as U.S. senator from Wyoming from 1979 to 1997.

He and his wife Ann celebrated their fiftieth wedding anniversary in 2004. The Simpsons have one daughter and two sons, both of whom are (you guessed it!) lawyers in (right again!) Cody, Wyoming. The Simpson family throughout its history has apparently followed another of Pericles's admonitions: "We do not say that a man who takes no interest in politics is a man who minds his own business. We say that he has no business here at all."

Senator Alan K. Simpson sent the following beautiful prayer:

> *Our Father, who has set a restlessness in our hearts, and made us all seekers after that which we can never fully find: Forbid us to be satisfied with what we make of life. Draw us from base content, and set our eyes on far off goals. Keep us at tasks too hard for us—that we may be driven to Thee for strength. Deliver us from fretfulness and self-pity; make us sure of the goal we cannot see and of the hidden good in the world. Open our eyes to simple beauty all around us, and our hearts to the loveliness men hide from us because we do not try enough to understand them. Save us from ourselves, and show us a vision of a world made new. May the Spirit of peace and illumination so enlighten our minds that all life shall glow with new meaning and new purpose.*

Senator Simpson was gracious enough to send an additional prayer before meals that he first heard from the Archbishop of Canterbury:

> *In a world filled with loneliness, thank you for our friends;*
> *In a world filled with hunger, thank you for our food.*

In a world filled with illness, thank you for our healing.
In a world filled with fear, thank you for our faith—
in God's name.

Scott Simpson –
U.S. Open golf champion

I have worked on this compilation of celebrity prayers for five years. I've spent hundreds of hours at the library and on the computer, looking for ways to contact famous people, requesting their favorite prayer. I have also spent a lot of money on printing and postage. During this time, I had to put my work on the back burner when my wife fought two cancer episodes and other illnesses.

So, truth be known, there have been several occasions when I felt like abandoning the project altogether. But I endured, mostly due to prayer responses like the one I received from Scott Simpson. I was moved by Scott's beautiful prayer, and then I came to his last sentence, where he said, "Chuck, my only hope is that God honors you for honoring Him." As tears welled up in my eyes, I got a renewed determination to see that this book of prayers got published. Then, perhaps other people could receive the inspiration all the prayers have brought to me.

Although the above paragraph doesn't tell you any statistical information on Scott Simpson, I think it does tell you a lot about the man. Both Scott's parents were elementary teachers, and Scott gets his golfing ability from his father. After winning the state junior title and coming in second in the U.S. junior championship, Scott accepted a scholarship from USC. At USC, his success continued as Scott won NCAA titles in both his junior and senior years.

During his professional career, he won six major trophies including the 1980 Western Open, 1984 Manufacturers Hanover Westchester Classic, the 1987 Greater Greensboro Open, and the 1989 Bell South Atlanta Classic. His favorite victories were the 1987 U.S. Open and the 1993 GTE Byron Nelson.

Through the personal influence of Morris Hatalsky and Larry Moody and the writings of Josh McDowell, Scott accepted Christ into his life in 1984.

Scott met Cheryl, his wife-to-be, in high school. They have two children.

This was the note and prayer I received from Scott Simpson:

Dear Chuck,

My favorite prayer is the one I say to God, and while similar, day to day, it's also personal and probably changes a bit. To me, prayer has always been about talking to God. So this is an example of how I personally pray, I suppose:

> *Dear Father, I know you are the most awesome creator*
> *of the universe and everything in it. You are good, you*
> *are great and beyond anything I can imagine. But you*
> *are also my father as I am your son, and I know that*

you care about everything I do, and that your love for me is even beyond my love for my children. You ask me to make my requests known to you, and I do that, knowing humbly how much you care for me. I ask that you watch over my wife, my kids, and myself. Help my kids to grow up knowing you, loving you, and desiring to please you in all they do. Help them know that in any circumstances, whether good or bad, that they have you to turn to for wisdom and help. Help us all be able to share your love with others. We know that you can make all things work together for your glory, and so I just ask that we can stay true to you through our triumphs, trials, and tragedies always knowing you are good, great, and in control. One day, evil will be gone, and we will be with you forever. We look forward to that day, and strive to make the best of our days here on earth until we're called home.

We thank you for this great country of America, and pray that people will turn to you for wisdom, because that's the only way we'll stay free and strong. We pray for the leaders of our country that they will remember that you are the truth, the way, and the life. We also pray for the people of the world, that they will lean on you if they already know you, and for those that don't, that you will touch them and show them that they need you above all else. That you offer them the free gift of eternal life if they'll just put their faith and trust in Jesus Christ.

So thank you for all of our blessings, and thank you for the trials that we learn from and gain strength from.

Most of all, we thank you for our Lord and Savior Jesus Christ, and the certain knowledge that we will be with you in a perfect heaven for all eternity. We love you, Lord, and thank you for loving us so much too.

Coach Dean Smith –
U. of North Carolina basketball coach

I spent the 1971-72 school year working toward my master's degree at West Virginia University in Morgantown. My wife took a part-time job during this time as a hostess at the Lakeview Country Club. It was my good fortune that the NCAA Eastern Regional Finals were played that year in the WVU Coliseum. And it was added good fortune that the Tar Heels of North Carolina stayed at Lakeview during the tournament.

I made sure that during the days of the tournament, I came an hour early to pick Patrice up from work. During this time, I sat in the lobby to catch a glimpse of Coach Dean Smith and his team. I enjoyed meeting several of the Tar Heel players, and I found them to be great representatives for their school. The team won the tournament but was defeated in the Final Four.

As I look back, I realize what legendary players were on that team—Bob McAdoo, Bobby Jones, George Karl, Dennis Wuycik, and Bill Chamberlain. Little did I know at the time that the team's

26-6 record would be the first of an NCAA record thirty-one consecutive seasons in which North Carolina would win twenty or more games! I did not know that by the year 1997, Coach Smith would become the NCAA's all-time winningest coach (879-254). Nor did I know that Smith's teams would go on to compile the all-time record (sixty-five) for most NCAA tournament victories. I did not know that his Tar Heels would finish first in the rugged ACC regular season a record seventeen times. I did not know that Coach Smith would become one of only four men to coach teams to NIT, NCAA, and Olympic championships*. I did not know that in 1997, he would be named *Sports Illustrated* Sportsman of the Year.

What I did know at the time is that Smith himself had been an accomplished basketball player and had played guard on the 1952 NCAA championship team for the Kansas Jayhawks.

There are any number of businesses and/or businesspeople who have paid millions of dollars to have a sports facility named in their honor. North Carolina's home court is named the Dean E. Smith Center (the "Dean Dome"). Coach Smith got this honor the old fashioned way: He earned it.

*the other three coaches were Bobby Knight, Adolph Rupp, and Pete Newell.

I was thrilled to receive a prayer from Coach Smith. His letter indicated that the prayer he sent was one that "we generally say at family time together:"

> *Our Creator, we once again pause to express our gratitude for your unconditional love and acceptance to us and all your human beings. Help each of us to*

*respond with ethical action in accepting and helping
people with whom we come in contact. Amen.*

Ellen Pasturzak Spinner –
Miss Ohio 1996

Ellen Pasturzak Spinner was born in the tiny rural town of
Otway, Ohio. Otway is near Portsmouth, which is separated from
the state of Kentucky by the Ohio River.

Ellen went to The Ohio State University, earned her B.A. in
nursing, and then her master's degree in women's health. In 1996,
as an OSU undergraduate, she won the title of Miss Ohio. In 1997,
she married our son, Scott. Although she has many talents and
titles, I think her greatest asset is the patience and love she shows
to her two young sons, Caleb and Joshua. The two boys were
named for the only two scouts sent out by Moses to come back
with favorable reports on the Promised Land. They were, therefore,
the only two scouts who were ultimately to be rewarded by being
able to enter the Land of Milk and Honey. In 2008 Ellen opened
the Gentle Care Health Facility in Mechanicsburg, Ohio.

Ellen wrote this note with her prayer:

"Dad, there are so many beautiful prayers—so many reminders of who and how I want to be. This one, from Mother Teresa, is my current favorite. I love this especially for where I am now in life's journey—building a home, buying a farm, raising two beautiful children; countless opportunities for others to cheat me, laugh at me—OR, countless opportunities for me to trust in others' goodness and expect great things—but at the very least, to take comfort in God's Grace working on me."

People are often
Unreasonable and self-centered:
Forgive them anyway.

If you are kind,
People may accuse you of ulterior motives:
Be kind anyway.

If you are honest,
People may cheat you:
Be honest anyway.

The good you do today
May be forgotten tomorrow:
Do good anyway.

Give the world the best you have,
And it may never be enough:
Give your best anyway.

For you see, in the end,
It is between you and God:
It never was between you and them anyway.

Scott Lee Spinner –
Dad Vail rowing champion

Of the more than 100 celebrity introductions I've had to write for this book, this one for our son Scott is without a doubt the toughest. Up until now, it's been relatively easy to put down historical facts for most of the people I am describing. But relaying a lifetime of feelings is quite a bit different. That's probably the reason why I've kept putting off this task. Scott's is the very last introduction I have had to compose. As they say, I have saved the best 'til last.

I could obviously write a book of stories about our Scott. He reminds me a lot of my dad, who had the knack of getting along with men and women of all ages, all shapes and sizes, and all social and economic statuses. He is sensitive, hard-working, and a good friend. But I think one of his most endearing qualities is his perseverance and determination.

People who meet Scott now probably think that this young man was born with a silver spoon in his mouth. He is handsome, has a beautiful, very personable wife, two handsome sons, and is a top salesman for Medline Industries. However, he has had to deal with his share of potential setbacks along the way

—Each year during his high school years at St. Ignatius High School in Cleveland, Ohio, Scott was one of the very last athletes to be cut from the basketball squad. He grudgingly gave in to the idea that a professional basketball career might not be in his future. However, he didn't withdraw from sports, he just found another avenue to success—and so he joined the school's crew team. He became quite a rower so that in his freshman year at Ohio's Marietta College his Novice 4 boat went undefeated (93-0) during the 1992 season and then went on to win the Dad Vail National Championships in Philadelphia.

—In grade school, tests showed that our son had epilepsy. He took medication to normalize this condition. During one summer vacation when he was in college, Scott had a seizure on the morning that he was to start his first day of construction. The doctor said that he could not work construction or drive a car for several months. On the way home from the doctor, Scott had his mother drive him to various business establishments within walking distance of our house. Within an hour, he had secured a summer job at our local BW3 restaurant. He again had found another avenue to achieve his goals.

—When Scott graduated from college in 1995, he was very anxious to become a success in the world of work. His first job with Cincinnati Bell Long Distance was abruptly interrupted two days before Christmas when the car he was driving was hit head-on by a drunk driver. It was only through the wearing of a seat belt, the protection provided by the air bag, a last nanosecond reflexive turn of the wheel, and the grace of God that Scott survived the crash that totally mangled his car.

Scott's injuries necessitated a long sabbatical from work and several operations. Scott knew that God saved him for a purpose and he worried that he might miss what that intention might be. He signed on as a member of the adult core group that guided the parish's youth group. And it was through this participation that he met Ellen Pasturzak, whom he would marry in 1997. Ellen and Scott have blessed Patrice and me with two wonderful grandkids, Caleb and Joshua. Joshua's middle name is "Ignatius" named for Scott's beloved Cleveland St. Ignatius High School.

☆   ☆   ☆

It is not a surprise to me that Scott's submission as his favorite prayer is from the writings of St. Ignatius of Loyola. It is called:

<u>Prayer for Generosity</u>
Lord, teach me to be generous,
Teach me to serve you as you deserve.
To give and not to count the cost,
To fight and not to heed the wounds,
To toil and not to seek for rest,
To labor and not to seek reward,
Save that of knowing that I do your will.

Dana Summers –
Political cartoonist/*Orlando Sentinel*

The notorious robber-baron, William Tweed, never bothered himself with attacking the muckrakers of the Populist Era. But he hated the editorial cartoonists. His reason? Tweed related that few of his immigrant constituents could read—but almost all of them could see!

As a social studies educator, I agreed with the power and efficacy of political cartoonists. "A picture is worth a thousand words," I would remind my students as I'd assign them to create their own cartoons on modern political and social issues.

Dana Summers is a popular contemporary political cartoonist for the *Orlando Sentinel*. Before working for the *Sentinel,* he drew for the *Dayton Journal Herald* in Ohio, and then for the *Fayetteville Times* in North Carolina.

Dana has been involved in the creation of two comic strips. The first of these, *The Middletons,* he co-created with Ralph Dunagin. His second strip, *Bound and Gagged,* is syndicated in 150 papers worldwide.

Dana has twice been awarded the Citation of Excellence by the Overseas Press Club. And he is a three-time winner of the Society of Professional Journalists/Sigma Delta Chi Southeast Award.

He and his wife Mary Jane live with their three children in Orlando, Florida.

Dana wrote: "Actually, my all-time favorite reading is the passage concerning the wedding feast at Cana!" (John 2:1-11) However, he thought that the passage might be a little too long for the book so he sent this prayer as well:

> *Oh Jesus, stretched out upon the cross, I implore You, give me the grace of doing faithfully the most holy will of Your Father, in all things, always and everywhere. And when this will of God will seem to me very harsh and difficult to fulfill, it is then I beg*

You, Jesus, may power and strength flow upon me from Your wounds, and may my lips keep repeating, "Your will be done, O Lord."

Jim Sundberg – Baseball player

When you reflect on all the great catchers who have ever played the game of baseball, you can come up with quite an outstanding list of athletes: Yogi Berra, Johnny Bench, Bill Dickey, Bill Freehan, Earl Battey, Mike Scioscia, Gabby Hartnett, and Del Crandell—to name just a few. But none of these catchers can match the durability exhibited by former major leaguer Jim Sundberg. Jim played more games at catcher for one team (1,927) than any of the above all stars.

Sundberg played sixteen seasons (1974-89) in the majors, most of these with the Texas Rangers, with short stints with the Milwaukee Brewers and the Kansas City Royals. He received the Gold Glove Award for his fielding ability six times and three times (1974, '78, and '84) he was named to the American League All-Star team.

Few people realize that just as Jim was beginning to establish himself in the major leagues, he broke his hip in 1975 and was out for the entire season. This injury makes Jim's longevity stats for number of games caught in a single season even more impressive. From 1971 through the 2003 season, only 123 major leaguers caught 90 percent or more of their team's games. Sundberg leads the list of iron man catchers for having accomplished this feat six times! Only 69 athletes in the entire history of the game have ever caught 140 or more games in a single season. Only thirty catchers have ever accomplished this more than once—*and Jim did it three times!* Not only did Jim play often at a difficult position—he played that position extremely well. In 1979, Jim set the American League record for the highest fielding percentage for a season (.995).

The Jim Sundberg Community Service Award was created in Jim's honor and is given annually to the most outstanding community volunteer in the north Texas area.

The statement that Jim sent is his life's purpose statement that he prays guides his life:

> *"I have concluded that all the accumulation of wealth, even if I could achieve it, is an insufficient reason for living. When I reach the end of my days, I must be able to look back on more than just Gold Gloves, All-Star games, World Championships, and records—nor is fame of any lasting benefit. I will consider my earthly existence to have been wasted unless I recall a loving family, a consistent investment in the lives of people, and an earnest attempt to serve the God who made me. And nothing else makes sense."*

Steve Tasker –
Seven-times selected to NFL Pro Bowl

When Steve Tasker was playing professional football, he was 5'9" tall and weighed 180 pounds. If you saw him on the street, you very well may not have been able to pick him out as a seven-time Pro Bowl selection. You may have skipped over him as one of only twenty-seven players the NFL Hall of Fame committee selected as the all-time best NFL players to have ever played the game!

Steve comes from a family of Methodist ministers. He grew up in Kansas and went to a junior college there before transferring to Northwestern University. Tasker was chosen in the ninth round of the 1985 draft by the Houston Oilers. He played there only a year and a half before the Buffalo Bills picked him up. Steve played on some great teams while in Buffalo, and his team went to four Super Bowls during his eleven and a half seasons with the Bills.

Steve earned a reputation as one of the best all-time special teams players in the league. He racked up 204 career special teams tackles, blocked seven punts, and was the only true special team's player to ever be named MVP of a Pro Bowl.

His only ejection in his career occurred two minutes into his final pro game against Green Bay when he bumped into an official when he was arguing a call. After his playing days were over in 1997, Steve had a smooth transition from playing sports to announcing them.

The Taskers have five children and the family is very involved in their local Methodist parish and activities.

☆   ☆   ☆

This is Steve's note that accompanied his special prayer: "Chuck, This is the prayer that I used to pray before each kick-off I would cover, while I would be lined up for the first kick-off of every game:"

> *God, thank you for this opportunity. Protect all of us from injury and I pray that this game glorifies you! Be with us all! Amen.*

Bobby Thomson –
Hit most famous home run in history

Bobby Thomson's 1951 walk-off home run that beat the New York Giants and propelled the Dodgers into the World Series has almost always been selected as one of baseball's all-time most important moments. Bobby's homer was immortalized by veteran announcer Russ Hodges's call. Eight times, Hodges shouted into the mike, "The Giants win the pennant!" as Thomson rounded the bases. We even know that Thomson's "shot heard around the world" took place at precisely 3:58 pm on October 3 and capped a remarkable late-season rally by the Giants, who had trailed the Dodgers by thirteen and a half games as late as August 12.

When Thomson came to the plate, the Giants were trailing 4-2 with one out in the bottom of the ninth. Immediately prior to Thomson's at-bat, the Giant's Don Mueller had injured his ankle sliding into third base and had to be attended to and eventually carried off the field. Then a pitching change was made. Ralph Branca replaced Don Newcombe. Thomson had hit a home run off Branca in the sixth inning of the first playoff game.

Thomson's home run has overshadowed the fact that the Giants ultimately lost the World Series four games to two to the New York Yankees.

Bobby was born in Glasgow in the UK and came to the U.S. when he was just two years old. Before he made the big leagues, he served as a bombardier in the U.S. Air Corps from 1943 to 1945. He lost the 1947 Rookie of the Year award to Jackie Robinson.

Few people remember that Bobby could have just as easily been remembered as the goat of that famous game for a running error he had made earlier in the game. Few people also remember that there was one out in the inning and had Thomson struck out, there was at least one more batter to come to the plate. That batter was rookie Willie Mays.

We are proud to have prayers not only from Bobby Thomson, but also from two other players who played in that classic game. Carl Erskine was also warming up in the bullpen when the Dodgers chose Branca to pitch to Thomson. The home run sailed over the head of Dodger left fielder Andy Pafko.

Bobby Thomson will always be known for his famous home run; but, after his baseball career, he—and Ralph Branca I might add—would be known for their positive contributions to their community.

Bobby Thomson wrote in response to our prayer request letter that "I don't have any favorite prayer when I speak to God. I ask for peace and love for my family and all peoples. I give thanks for everything I have in life and ask for strength that I may help others."

Lonnie Melvin "Mel" Tillis – Singer/actor

Mel Tillis is one of our country's most talented and endearing singer/songwriters. His fans know what an inspiration he has been to countless persons who have suffered from any form of speech impediment. Tillis is said to have started to stutter after an episode of malaria at the age of three. However, as with many people encountering this problem, when Mel sang, there was nothing but pure, flowing tones.

In 1951, after high school, Mel entered the service. While he was in Okinawa, Japan, serving as a baker, he formed a band called the Westerners.

Upon returning to the States after his term in the military, he first broke into the music business as a songwriter. In 1957, Webb Pierce took Mel's song, "I'm Tired" to number three on the country charts. The first successful song that Tillis himself recorded was "The Violet and a Rose," which hit number twenty-four in 1958. Throughout his career, Mel has penned some wonderful songs performed by other artists, such as: "Detroit City" (Bobby Bare), "Ruby, Don't Take Your Love to Town" (Kenny Rogers), "Emotions" (Brenda Lee), "Snakes Crawl Out at Night" (Charley Pride), "One More Time" (Ray Price), "Mary, Don't You Weep" (Stonewall Jackson), "Mental Revenge" (Waylon Jennings), "Honey, Open That Door" (Ricky Skaggs), and "Diggin' Up Bones" (Randy Travis).

In 1972, Mel finally recorded his first very own number-one hit with "I Ain't Never." Throughout his career, Mel has written more than 1,000 songs, recorded more than sixty albums, sixty-seven top-forty hits, and nine number-one hits!

He also has appeared in some classic comedy films such as: *WW and the Dixie Dancekings, The Villain, Every Which Way but Loose, Smokey and the Bandit II,* and both *Cannonball Run* films.

Since the 1990s, Tillis has been one of the most popular performers at Branson, Missouri. Mel has six children, one of whom, Pam Tillis, is a top country recording artist in her own right.

Mel Tillis sent an adaptation of the Serenity Prayer as his favorite prayer. He mentioned that it used to help him with his stuttering.

> *Oh Lord, Grant me the courage to change the things*
> *I can change, the serenity to accept those I cannot*

change, and wisdom to know the difference. And God,
Grant me the courage to not give up on what I think
is right, even though I think it is hopeless.

Jacquelyn Mayer Townsend –
Miss America 1963

Our daughter-in-law, Ellen, and Jackie Mayer Townsend will forever share a common bond. They both were named Miss Ohio (Jackie in 1963 and Ellen in 1996). Jackie, however, took the next step that only three other Miss Ohios have taken: She was named Miss America. I should note here that Ohio has the distinction of having the only Miss America to have ever won the title twice, Mary Katherine Campbell (1922-23).

As a history teacher, I have always admired people who have overcome what appeared to be overwhelming odds. I admire Mrs. Townsend because of how she battled back from her 1970 debilitating stroke. It was not easy, and it took Jackie five years to relearn the alphabet, numbers, and to regain the ability to talk.

It was not enough for her to overcome the adversity that confronted her. She felt that she could be an example for others who might have to face the same challenge. Jackie became a charter board member of the National Stroke Association, and a rehabilitation center at Providence Hospital in Sandusky, Ohio is named in her honor.

Jackie and her husband, John, have two children, Bill and Kelly.

Mrs. Townsend wrote that "I love the Psalm (16:8) that begins, 'I have set the Lord always before me, because He is at my right hand, I shall not be moved.' I have used this since before I was Miss America. It has given me such peace."

Jackie also related that she used to work for the Sisters of St. Francis at Providence Hospital. Although she is not Catholic, Jackie indicated that she appreciated the love and blessings that St. Francis of Assisi gave to so many generations. She had the opportunity to travel to Assisi and the prayer of St. Francis is also a favorite of hers.

Prayer of St. Francis

Lord Jesus, make me an instrument of your peace.
Where there is hatred, Let me sow Love.
Where there is injury, Pardon.
Where there is doubt, Faith.
Where there is despair, Hope.
Where there is darkness, Light.
And where there is sadness, Joy.
O Divine Master,
Grant that I may not so much seek
To be consoled as to console,
To be understood as to understand,
To be loved as to love.
For it is in giving that we receive,
It is in pardoning that we are pardoned,
And it is in dying that we are born to eternal life.

Fred Travalena –
Singer/impersonator

Fred is known as "The Man of a Thousand Faces," "Mr. Everybody," and "The Olivier of Comedy" for the number and quality of his impersonations. Although he can imitate many celebrities, I believe he is especially known for his tributes to our nation's presidents who have served from 1960 to the present. Fred was a guest at George H.W. Bush's presidential inauguration in 1989. At that time, the president signed a photograph of Fred made up like George Bush with the inscription, "To Me, George Bush."

Travalena is blessed with a three-octave singing range. So, although he is known for impersonating the singing style of the likes of Frank Sinatra, he has become an accomplished singer and songwriter in his own right.

Fred has been a guest on many talk shows and game shows. His versatility has allowed him to act in movies and perform on comedy specials.

This popular entertainer has been active in a variety of causes, most notably working on behalf on POW and MIA families, cerebral palsy, juvenile diabetes, YWCA, and the Arthritis Foundation.

The prayer that Fred Travalena sent was written by Fred and Pastor John Steward for "National Reconciliation Day," November 8, 1992. It is based on 2 Chronicles 7:14-15. Let us pray:

Oh God, we come to you today and we ask for your help.

We ask you, oh God, to bring about renewal and change in this world. We're coming to you today to ask for forgiveness and renewal in our lives. We ask you for forgiveness for the misuse and damage that we have done to the environment, to the earth, to the air, and to the water.

(In your mercy, oh God, hear our prayer.)

For the mistreatment and the abuse of animals that often results in death, forgive us, Lord.

(In your mercy, oh God, hear our prayer.)

For the misuse of our nation's financial blessing, for violation of public trust, for unlawful testimony, for our misuse of all you have given us, forgive us, Lord.

(In your mercy, oh God, hear our prayer.)

For not fulfilling our responsibilities to the children of the earth, for child abuse, for the starvation of millions of children, for the lack of clothing and medicine and education for children, forgive us, Lord.

(In your mercy, oh God, hear our prayer.)

For the sins of racial bigotry and prejudice, and for religious intolerance, forgive us, Lord.

(In your mercy, oh God, hear our prayer.)

For intolerance toward those who are our fellow citizens on this planet, for intolerance against African Americans, Asian Americans, Native Americans—against all your children, forgive us, Lord.

(In your mercy, oh God, hear our prayer.)

For the unjust taking of human life, for substance abuse, for violations of your commandments, forgive us, Lord.

(In your mercy, oh God, hear our prayer.)

For lack of kindness and compassion for one another, forgive us, Lord.

(In your mercy, oh God, hear our prayer.)

Father, we come to you in this moment of silence, bringing you our petitions, reconciling ourselves with you and with one another, we are asking for our beloved soldiers (MIAs) to be set free. Father, we are seeking to learn how to forgive and to be forgiven, and our prayer today is that by learning how to forgive, this might create a spiritual renewal in our land. We need to learn how to love one another and we need to embrace a broken world. And if we do, oh God, our

*prayer is that you will set the prisoners free. We ask
this in your Holy name oh Jesus. Amen.*

Jim Tressel –
Ohio State football coach

When I came to Cleveland in 1968, I couldn't tell you who the
mayor of Berea, Ohio was. But, I soon came to recognize that Lee
Tressel, the man with the crew cut and bow tie, was the coach of
Baldwin Wallace College's (Berea, Ohio) football team.

Young Jim Tressel would quarterback for his father's team and
then spend fifteen years himself as a head coach at Youngtown
State. At YSU, Tressel compiled a 135-57-2 record while winning
four Division 1-AA national championships (1991, '93, '94, and
'97). Lee and Jim Tressel are the only father-son combination to
win national football championships. Jim was named Division
1-AA Coach of the Year three times.

Coach Tressel then took over the reins at Ohio State in 2001.
OSU went 7-5 that first year (highlighted by a win at Michigan).
The next year, when the Buckeyes went 14-0 and won the national
championship, Tressel was again named national coach of the year.

Only the Bowden family (Bobby, Tommy, and Terry) has more
college wins than do the Tressels (Lee, Jim, and Jim's brother,
Dick).

Jim Tressel always remembers his father's deep concern for his players. That characteristic of the father seems to have passed down to his son and is a major factor in his success.

Coach Tressel and his wife Ellen have four children.

☆   ☆   ☆

Coach Tressel's favorite prayer is a reflection written by David Livingstone:

> *Lord, send me anywhere,*
> *Only go with me.*
> *Lay any burden on me,*
> *Only sustain me.*
> *Sever any tie but the tie*
> *That binds me to Thyself.*

Virgil "Fire" Trucks – Detroit Tigers pitcher

Only four pitchers in all of major league history have hurled two no-hitters in a single season: Nolan Ryan, Johnny Van DerMeer, Allie Reynolds, and Virgil "Fire" Trucks. Few people know that two unusual things are associated with the year that Trucks recorded his rare feat.

First, in his next pitching assignment after throwing his first no-hitter of the 1952 season, Virgil retired twenty-six batters in a row after giving up a lead-off single with his first pitch of the game!

Secondly, Trucks's no-hitters came in a season when his overall record was a dismal five wins and nineteen losses! In his five victories, Virgil gave up only nine hits!

Virgil Trucks won 177 games in his career. He probably would have won quite a few more contests had he played for better teams and had his career not been interrupted for military service. Just two weeks after being discharged from the navy, Virgil won a complete game victory in Game 2 of the 1945 World Series! Trucks calls this achievement a bigger thrill than either of his two no-hitters. The Tigers pitchers—Trout, Newhouser, and Trucks—were collectively known as "TNT." Remarkably, Virgil completed 124 games and recorded 33 shutouts in his years in professional baseball. Virgil was selected to the American League All-Star squad in 1949 and 1954.

Here is the favorite prayer that Virgil Trucks sent:

Father,
Thank you for the many blessings, forgive me of all my sins, and
bless me, my wife, and our families. Bless the poor, sick, and
homeless people.
Most of all, bless the children of the world
so they may have food for all
and guidance to a happy and righteous life.
Amen.

Bishop Desmond Mpilo Tutu – Nobel Peace Prize recipient

Desmond Mpilo Tutu was educated at Johannesburg Bantu High School. His father was a teacher, and at first, it seemed that Desmond would follow this career path when, after college, he returned to teach three years at his old school. However, Desmond left teaching, studied theology, and in 1960 was ordained an Anglican priest. He received his master's degree in theology in 1966 from King's College in London, England.

Reverend Tutu taught theology in South Africa and always advocated the rights of the oppressed. In 1975, he was appointed Dean of St. Mary's Cathedral in Johannesburg. The next year, he was became bishop of Lesotho. And, when in 1978, Bishop Tutu was made secretary general of the South African Council of Churches, his opinions took on the added influence of that position. In 1984, the bishop and his lifetime of work was recognized when he was awarded the Nobel Peace Prize.

Archbishop Tutu has been married to Leah Nomalizo since 1955. The couple has four children: Trevor Thamsanga, Theresa Thandeka, Naomi Nontombi, and Mpho Andrea.

Archbishop Tutu continues to teach by lecturing and writing, and through it all, presents the message of acceptance and promotes the dignity and worth of all men and women. This goal is evident in the prayer he sent for the book:

Goodness is stronger than evil.
Light is stronger than darkness.
Love is stronger than hate.
Victory is ours through Him who loves us.
Amen.

Marilyn Van Derbur – Miss America 1958

Our wonderful daughter-in-law, Ellen, was chosen as Miss Ohio in 1996. She then participated in the Miss America pageant held in Atlantic City, New Jersey. After I received a favorite prayer from Marilyn Van Derbur, Miss America 1958, I asked Ellen if she'd ever heard of Miss Van Derbur. Without a second's hesitation, Ellen replied that she certainly had!

As part of the Miss America competition, there is always a part of the judging where each contestant is put on the spot with a challenging question. The year our Ellen was involved in the pageant, former Miss Americas were invited back to ask the girls their questions. And, of all of the possible match-ups, our Ellen was selected to be paired with Marilyn Van Derbur! Small world—right?!

Marilyn's history seems to be able to be divided into several sections. The first is what seemed like an idyllic childhood. Marilyn and her three sisters were the daughters of a very prominent Denver businessman. Marilyn studied at the University of Colorado. In her sophomore year, she was crowned Miss Colorado, and subsequently Miss America. She went on to graduate and, in fact, earned Phi Beta Kappa honors.

But, all was not well. Marilyn was hiding a secret that was masked by what appeared to others as a gifted life. It wasn't until 1991 that Marilyn revealed that she had been the victim of incest by her father from when she was five years old until she was eighteen. For years, Marilyn suffered mentally and physically from this trauma. She has found peace only by bringing the issue to the level of consciousness, confronting her father, helping to establish an adult survivor program in Denver, co-founding two national organizations to protect child victims of sexual abuse, producing twenty-four films, and, in 2004, writing *Miss America by Day: Lessons Learned from Ultimate Betrayals and Unconditional Love*. At the Eleventh Annual Writer's Digest International Self-Published Book Awards, her book was awarded first place in the inspirational section out of 242 books in that category!

Marilyn personally responded to my prayer request. At the time, I was quite frustrated with my apparent inability to get my book of prayers published. Marilyn gave me encouragement by telling me that she self-published her book and suggested perhaps I could do the same. Ultimately, that is the path I have taken.

Marilyn and her husband Larry Atler have one child, Jennifer.

I was delighted to have Marilyn Van Derbur Atler share with us this beautiful prayer:

> *Lord, I crawled across the barrenness to You*
> *with my empty cup, uncertain in asking*
> *any small drop of refreshment.*
> *If only I had known You better,*
> *I'd have come running with a bucket.*

Richard J. "Dick" Vitale –
Sports announcer

"He's awesome, baby!"

Yes, we're talking about ESPN basketball announcer, Dick Vitale. Dicky V. is known for his enthusiastic broadcasts, his knowledge of the sport, his charity work, and his unique on-air lexicon. For example: "Get a T.O. (time out), baby," "a PTPer (prime time player)," "M & Mer" (a mismatch); "diaper dandy" (talented freshman); "Maalox time" (exciting last minutes of a game).

People would probably be surprised to discover that, after graduation from Seton Hall University, Vitale's first job was teaching at Mark Twain Elementary School. He then went on to win two state championships while teaching and coaching at his alma mater, East Rutherford High School in New Jersey. From 1973 to 1977, Dick became a head basketball coach at the University of Detroit. While there, he compiled a 78-30 record that included a twenty-one-game win streak. During that run (1976-77), his team defeated the eventual NCAA champ Marquette team coached by Al McGuire. Vitale was not as successful during his short tenure (78-79) with the Detroit Pistons and he was released early into the second year of his contract.

From coaching, Dicky V. was hired by fledgling sports station, ESPN, and he announced their very first NCAA collegiate broadcast (DePaul 90-Wisconsin 77) on December 5, 1979. Since that time, Vitale has broadcast more than 1,000 games for ESPN.

Since my wife has had two episodes of cancer, I am particularly impressed by Vitale's dedicated service to the V Foundation. This non-profit organization, founded in 1993 by ESPN and the late Jimmy Valvano, is dedicated to battling malignant melanoma/skin cancers.

Dick and his wife Lorraine have two daughters who earned their MBAs from Notre Dame, where they also played tennis.

You can tell that Dicky V. enjoys life and works at making a positive contribution to his community. As of this writing, Vitale has appeared in seven movies and has written seven books. Dick is on the selection committee for both the Naismith and Wooden awards and he also is a member of the Associated Press panel that ranks the top twenty-five men's basketball teams in the country.

He and Lorraine are involved in a remarkable number of charities.

Along with several brochures urging support for the V Foundation, Dick Vitale sent me his favorite prayer, the Prayer to St. Jude, that he noted he said every morning and evening.

195

<u>Prayer to St. Jude</u>

St. Jude, glorious Apostle, faithful servant and friend of Jesus, the name of the traitor has caused you to be forgotten by many, but the true Church invokes you universally as the Patron of things despaired of; pray for me, that finally I may receive the consolations and the succor of Heaven in all my necessities, tribulations and sufferings, particularly (here make your request), and that I may bless God with the Elect throughout Eternity.
Amen.

Senator George Victor Voinovich – U.S. Senator from Ohio

Even though I am a registered Democrat, I love Ohio's Republican Senator George Voinovich. Although I was born and raised in Illinois, I moved to Cleveland, Ohio in 1968. And it seems as if George Voinovich's involvement in Cleveland politics started at nearly the same time and he's been representing the citizens of Cleveland and Ohio ever since.

George won the trust of the people by working from the bottom up and proving himself to the people at each step along the way:

1967-71 Ohio House of Representatives
1971-76 Cuyahoga County Auditor
1977-78 Cuyahoga County Commissioner

1979-89 Mayor of Cleveland

1991-98 Governor of Ohio

1999-Senator of Ohio

Clevelanders especially appreciate George Voinovich because he became our mayor at a time when the city was in default and the butt of jokes nationwide. Clevelanders so loved their new mayor that, in 1981, they voted to extend the term of that office from two years to four. And in 1982, Cleveland was selected that year as one of only ten U.S. cities to be designated as an All-American city.

I also have a special place in my heart for Senator and Mrs. Voinovich for another reason. In 1995, our only child was hit head-on by a drunk driver. Our son survived. But I have through the years prayed for the Voinovich family, whose nine-year-old daughter, Molly, died in a traffic accident in 1978.

Having been a history teacher, I know that in 1885, Teddy Roosevelt lost both his wife and his mother on the same day. Yet, instead of withdrawing angrily from society, TR was his most active and productive in the years immediately following this tragedy. And so too it was with George and Janet Voinovich. Their public service contributions surely are an inspiration and a testimony to the memory of their daughter.

One of Senator Voinovich's favorite prayers that he turns to most for inspiration is from Isaiah 40:31:

> *But they that wait upon the Lord shall renew their strength; they shall mount up with wings as eagles; they shall run, and not be weary; and they shall walk, and not be faint.*

Mort Walker –
Cartoonist ("Beetle Bailey")

Mort Walker knew he wanted to be a cartoonist at the age of three when his father used to read the comic strips to him. By the age of fifteen, he created *The Lime Juices,* his first comic strip that was sold to a newspaper, the *Kansas City Journal.*

He worked nights at Hall Brothers (called Hallmark Cards since 1954) while he was attending college. In 1943, he was drafted and served in the army in Europe until the war ended in 1945.

In 1950, his most famous strip, *Beetle Bailey,* appeared in twelve newspapers. Few people know that "Beetle" was originally called "Spider" and was a student at the fictional Rockview University. By 1951, the strip and its main character changed to "Beetle Bailey." The cartoon has had obvious staying power and now appears internationally in more than 1,800 newspapers.

During his career, Mort Walker has created nine separate strips, four of which are still running:

Beetle Bailey (1950)

Hi and Lois (Lois is Beetle Bailey's sister!)

Boner's Ark (1968)

Sam and Silo (1977)

In 1974, Walker established the International Museum of Cartoon Art which is located in New York. Walker has been married to his second wife, Cathy, since 1985. Between them they have ten children, six of whom help produce the comic strips.

The University of Missouri, Walker's alma mater, honored Mort in 1992 by erecting a life-sized sculpture of his likeness on their campus.

In 2000, the U.S. Army awarded Mort its highest civilian honor, the Distinguished Civilian Service Award.

☆　　☆　　☆

Mort Walker submitted this prayer which, not surprisingly, is coming from the mouth of "Sarge:"

DEAR GOD,
  PLEASE HELP ME BE
MORE KIND AND UNDERSTANDING
WITH TOLERANCE AND COMPASSION,
CONTROLLING MY TEMPER AND
NEVER RESORTING TO VIOLENCE,
ALL OF THE ABOVE WITH ONE
  EXCEPTION ___ BEETLE

MORT WALKER ©KFS

Rusty Wallace –
Race car driver

My daughter-in-law, Ellen Pasturzak Spinner, is from deep in southern Ohio (Otway). After church on Sundays, it was natural for our family up in Cleveland to come home and watch the Browns on TV. It was just as natural for Ellen's family, when they returned from their church service, to gather to watch NASCAR races.

Voted one of the top fifty drivers in NASCAR's history is Rusty Wallace. It's not easy for a young driver to break into the Winston Cup circuit winner's circle. Although he was voted Rookie of the Year in 1984, it took Rusty seventy-two races before he won his first checkered flag, at Bristol Motor Speedway in the Valleydale 500 in April of 1986. It took Rusty 110 races before he won his first Winston Cup pole position in the 1987 Miller 400 at the Michigan International Speedway.

Since those early days, Rusty has accumulated quite a racing record:

- 1989 NASCAR Winston Cup Series Champion
- 1988 and 1993 NMPA Driver of the Year

- Fifty-four career Winston Cup wins, with thirty on super-speedways
- Thirty-six career Winston Cup poles, with twenty-two on super-speedways
- His fifty-four career wins and three career poles rank him tied for eighth place all-time in both categories
- His sixteen consecutive seasons with at least one race win ranks third all-time behind only Richard Petty (eighteen years) and David Pearson (seventeen years)
- First winner in modern-day NASCAR Winston Cup international competition by winning in Suzuka City, Japan, on November 24, 1996
- Career earnings of over $39 million ranks fifth all-time

His most embarrassing moment in racing occurred when he crashed while waving to fans during a victory lap in Springfield, Missouri.

Rusty is a jet-rated pilot and he owns his own airplane and helicopter.

Rusty lives with his wife, Patti, and their three children in the Charlotte, North Carolina area.

Here's Rusty's short but practical and purposeful prayer:

Dear God,
I know I messed up a lot, but please bail me out of this one!

Kurt Warner –
Two-time NFL MVP

My mother used to tell us kids that a person's character is determined by how they accept the bad as well as the good that would inevitably come our way. Sometimes, when we look at celebrities, we tend to think that life has always been easy for them and we tend to overlook the setbacks that they may have had to overcome. A perfect example of a celebrity whose faith has carried him through both the thrill of victory and the agony of defeat is pro football player Kurt Warner.

His parents divorced when Kurt was just four years old. He sat on the bench until his last year of football at Northern Iowa. Every pro team passed him up in the college draft. He therefore spent some time after college stocking shelves for minimum wage at the local grocery store. He had to work his way into the pros by first playing arena football and then competing in the European Football League. He missed a tryout with the Chicago Bears because of a swollen elbow caused by a spider bite. The parents of the woman he was dating (his future wife, Brenda) were both killed in an Arkansas tornado.

Despite these setbacks, Kurt has always decided to put first things first. (In fact, First Things First is the name that Kurt and Brenda gave to the foundation they established to promote Christian values and to help the needy.) By *first things first,* Kurt means "faith" and "family."

And that emphasis has helped Kurt appreciate and be thankful for the many positive moments that have also come along in his life. When he got the opportunity to play his last year at Northern Iowa, he made the best of it and was named the Gateway Conference Offensive Player of the Year. He led the Iowa Barnstormers of the Arena Football League to the Arena Bowl two straight years. When he played for the Amsterdam Admirals, he was tops in NFL Europe in passing yardage and touchdowns. As a starter for the St. Louis Rams, Kurt played in the Pro Bowl three straight years. He quarterbacked the Rams to two Super Bowls and was the league MVP two years (1999 and 2001). After his stint with the New York Giants, he signed a contract with the Arizona Cardinals.

Kurt Warner has a refreshing, positive attitude toward life. At the times in his life he has been handed lemons, he has quickly turned them into lemonade, which he has unselfishly shared with those who are thirsty.

Kurt and Brenda have five children.

Of all the responses that have been sent in, I was extremely impressed by Kurt Warner's prayer. Not only did he send in a sample of one of his prayers, but he then analyzed the elements that he always included when he talks to the Lord. I felt that these notes were particularly helpful as a model for prayer.

Dear Heavenly Father,
I humbly approach your throne asking your forgiveness[1] for
all my shortcomings, daily mistakes, and deliberate acts of

disobedience. I enter your presence in awe of your tremendous grace and mercy upon me. Praise and thanksgiving[2] are forever on my lips and in my heart for the daily blessings you bestow upon me. I thank you for your call[3] on my life and I ask for continual wisdom[4] to be able to fulfill this call perfectly, being boldly unashamed and without hesitation.[5] Lord, I long to see your face in every area of my life. Please, make yourself known[6] to me today like never before. Help me to know you more intimately, growing in understanding of the length, width, height and depth of your love for me.[7]
In Jesus' Name. Amen

Note: What follows is Kurt's note that accompanied his prayer:

"I don't have any set prayers I repeat during my prayer times, but I would say I have an outline of the specific areas I try to address within my daily quiet time with Jesus. Although, the depth and details may vary daily, in the above prayer I have numbered these areas:

1) I always come to God asking and accepting FORGIVENESS to Restore my perfect position.
2) I enter a state of WORSHIP, reminding myself of His greatness
3) I address MY UNIQUE PLACE in his plan
4) I ask for WISDOM to help me fulfill my purpose
5) I ask for STRENGTH in my WITNESS for Him
6) I ask for Him to SHOW HIS FACE to me every day of my life
7) I ask for help in GROWING CLOSER in my RELATIONSHIP with Him."

Thelma Wells –
One of leaders of Women of Faith

"In Christ, I can BEE the Best"

Thelma Wells is one of the six core members (along with Patsy Clairmont, Nicole Johnson, Marilyn Meberg, Luci Swindoll, and Sheila Walsh) of the very popular Christian organization, Women of Faith, which was founded in 1996.

Thelma wears a bumblebee pin every day as a reminder of the message of encouragement that insect imparts. Thelma best describes the significance of the bumblebee on her Web site: "… I am amazed that the bumblebee is able to do what God designed it to do in spite of its scientific limitations. You see, the body of a bumblebee is too big, [and] its wingspan too narrow for it to be able to fly. Yet it flies around anyway doing what God made it to do. It defies the laws of aeronautical science but adheres to the law of God!"

Beside her busy schedule speaking at the Women of Faith conferences, Thelma is the founder and president of the Daughters of Zion Leadership Mentoring Program as well as president of A Woman of God Ministries. She also somehow has found time to write numerous books and magazine articles.

Thelma holds a master's of divinity degree in pastoral ministry and has spoken in all fifty states, as well as nineteen foreign countries.

She and her husband George have three children, ten grandchildren, and one great-grandchild.

I was honored that immediately after returning from one of her conferences, Thelma composed, and sent me this profoundly beautiful prayer for the book:

Father in Heaven,

Your name is Holy, Awesome, Majestic, the Only God of the universe. How I bless Your name. How I lean upon your everlasting arms to hold me, comfort me, and lift me up. How I depend on Your word for wisdom and knowledge. How I honor Your precepts. My heart is filled with gratitude for all the good and perfect gifts You give me, even the gifts of situations and circumstances that I don't want and don't like. Yet, I've learned through these six decades that Your ways are all good for me when I allow You to have Your way. You've brought me through heartache and sorrow, through disappointment and disillusionment, through sickness and disease, through poverty and pain. But, through it all, I've learned to trust You. I've gotten closer to You. I know You keep Your promises.

Help me, Lord, to continue to be patient when I pray to You for things and people. Help me to remain peaceful and content when I can't see You moving in my circumstances. Move me out of Your way and help me to put You on my mind. Thank you for reminding me that when I don't know what to pray or how to pray I can always pray Your name, 'Jesus, Jesus, Jesus.' There is power in the name of Jesus!

Father, I pray for our nation and the leaders of our nation that they will be led by You and You alone. Please cover our men in the armed services with Your protection and bring them home soon from the battlefields in the world. Help the decisions of the President of the United States to be discerning and wise and for the betterment of all peoples. Within our state and local governments, give us people of high moral character and fervor for You, God.

Families are in need to You. Please, Lord, rebuke the enemies of our families that are trying to destroy the sanctity of the home, the obedience of children, the honor of parents and love in relationships. May jealousy and rivalry be overthrown by unity and oneness. Cause family members to hold each other up and encourage each other with tenderness and grace.

Millions of people have either never heard of You, Lord, or they've heard and not understood. Help me to be a more vital conduit of Your love, mercy, grace, kindness, and message of salvation to a world of people who do not know You. Father, help my light to shine before men that they will see You in me and want what I have, the saving knowledge of Jesus. Draw them into Your loving safety zone so they can qualify for an abundant life on the earth and life eternal in heaven. Help us all seek a relationship with You, not a religion about You.

There are those who are sick, incarcerated, abused, depressed, abandoned, deprived, rejected, homeless and helpless. You know who they are. Show me what I can do to assist. Cover them with Your protection and give them a way out of their horrible predicaments.

Now, Lord, there is much to pray for that's running in my head. Thank God, You know exactly what I want to pray for. The Holy Spirit understands my groanings. I trust You to answer. I will wait on You, Holy Father. I will keep my mind on You so You will keep me in perfect peace.

May this prayer be for Your glory and honor.

In Jesus' name, Amen.

Father Robert Welsh, SJ – President/Cleveland St. Ignatius High School

My wife and I first met Father Welsh in 1988 when our son enrolled at Cleveland St. Ignatius High School. As president of the high school, Father spoke calmly and eloquently as he welcomed the parents of the class of 1991.

Robert was the youngest of six children. His father was a lawyer/bailiff at Cleveland's municipal court. Of his father, Father Welsh asserts, "I've never met a finer man." And he idolized his mother.

Father relates that he was blessed with a clarity of vision at an early age of knowing what he wanted his life to become. He received his master's degree in history and theology from Loyola University in 1968. As president of Ignatius High School from 1979 to 2000, he was able to give kids the opportunity to love and serve Jesus Christ. Welsh's accomplishments were achieved through a focus, purpose, and a tenacity of spirit. In the year 2000, the school awarded him its most prestigious Magis Award for distinguished service to the church and to St. Ignatius.

Today, Father Welsh continues his service to youth in his position as vice president of mission at St. Martin de Porres High School. This inner-city Cleveland school is one of eleven such schools in the country that teaches students four days a week and has one day for enrollees to co-op in offices at entry-level jobs.

To me and my family Father Welsh is a celebrity, albeit a local one. He hasn't saved any major league baseball games; but, he is striving to save something much more important.

I believe that Father Welsh's life is a perfect embodiment of his favorite prayer, which not surprisingly is "The Prayer for Generosity" from St. Ignatius Loyola:

Lord,
Teach me to be generous,
Teach me to serve you as you deserve:
To give and not to count the cost,
To fight and not to heed the wounds,
To toil and not to seek for rest,
To labor and not to ask for any reward,
Except to know that I do your will.
Amen.

Dr. Robert White – Cleveland neurosurgeon

I know Dr. Robert White only through his reputation and through biographical articles. I do know his son and daughter-in-law, as friends and former teaching colleagues at Shaker Heights High School in Shaker Heights, Ohio.

Dr. White, is a reknown physician who recently retired after also teaching forty years at Case Western Reserve University as an instructor of neurological surgery.

White has had an illustrious career, and has practiced medicine and lectured throughout the world. He is a devout Catholic and in 1994 was appointed to the Pontifical Academy of Sciences, a Vatican advisory body.

Dr. White is known for his controversial methods and experiments to achieve medical advances. His research has led to discussions such as:

- the extent and future advances in transplantation
- the method of placing the brain into hypothermia during an operation
- the importance of the brain as a center perhaps of the soul as well as the mind.

☆   ☆   ☆

Professor White's favorite prayer is the Hail Mary:

Hail Mary, full of grace, the Lord is with thee.
Blessed art thou among women,
And blessed is the fruit of thy womb, Jesus.
Holy Mary, Mother of God,
Pray for us sinners,
Now and at the hour of our death.
Amen.

Dr. Walter Wink –
Minister, professor, author

During the summer following his sophomore year at Southern Methodist University, Walter Wink journeyed out to Oregon (from Dallas) to be off on his own and to examine his faith. He ended up working at a lumber yard, then picking strawberries and cherries, and finally stocking and cleaning up at a furniture store. During that summer, Walter experienced a spiritual transformation that would help guide his future as a Methodist pastor and professor.

During the summer of my junior year in college, I too journeyed west to California (from Chicago). I was in a seminary and wanted to be more independent so as to more clearly examine the path I would pursue in the coming years. During my summer adventure (during which time I also picked strawberries!), I also made a decision: My vocation would indeed be one of service, but as a high school history instructor.

I can therefore appreciate the journey that Walter took during his youth. Sometimes we need to get away to get closer to God.

Dr. Wink went on to receive his Th.D. from Union Theological Seminary in New York. He then served as a pastor of a church near Houston for five years. In 1967, he returned to teach at his alma mater. Dr. Wink was very affected by the peace movement taking place at that time and in 1989-1990 he was made a Peace Fellow at the United States Institute of Peace.

Dr. Wink is Professor Emeritus at New York City's Auburn Theological Seminary, where his wife, June Keener Wink is an adjunct faculty member. Dr. Wink is a prolific author on theology and biblical studies.

Dr. Wink's contribution comes from his book *Engaging the Powers: Discernment and Resistance in a World of Domination* (Fortress Press 1992), p. 308:

"Many, especially in Alcoholics Anonymous, have been greatly helped by the prayer attributed to one of my teachers, Reinhold Niebuhr: "God, grant me the serenity to accept the things I cannot change, the courage to change the things I can, and the wisdom to know the difference." ... I would prefer to pray, "God, help me to refuse ever to accept evil; by your Spirit empower me to work for change precisely where and how you call me; and free me from thinking I have to do everything."

John Wooden –
Legendary UCLA basketball coach

In writing this book, I tried to "be quick, but don't hurry." It is one of my all-time best quotes from Coach Wooden.

John Wooden's amazing basketball coaching record can be attributable to the following traits: a knowledge of the game, tremendous organizational skills, hard work, and a life centered in prayer and principles. Coach Wooden compiled records that will last for the ages. During his twenty-six years as head basketball coach of the UCLA Bruins, he had:

- four 30-0 seasons

- eighty-eight consecutive victories

- nineteen PAC 10 championships

- a 149-2 record at Pauley Pavilion
- thirty-eight straight NCAA tournament victories
- ten national champions with seven of them being consecutive

It took time and effort to build such a record at UCLA. Coach Wooden kept a three-by-five note card of every practice his teams ever held. On the first days of practice, he coached the fundamentals, which even included how to put on one's socks so as to prevent blisters. It wasn't until his fifteenth season with the Bruins that his "Pyramid of Success" fully took hold and he won his first national championship.

Few people realize that the "Wizard of Westwood" was quite an accomplished player in his own right. In high school in Indiana, he lettered all four years, won All-State honors his last three years (1926-1928), and helped his team get to the Indiana State Championship those same three years (they won it all in 1927).

At Purdue, the All-American guard led the Boilermakers to two Big 10 titles and the 1932 national championship.

If few people know of the coach's stellar playing career, fewer still know that after college, he coached high school basketball and taught English for nine years. And fewer still know that Wooden then served as a full lieutenant in the U.S. Navy from 1943 to 1946.

Coach Wooden adored his wife, Nell, to whom he was married for fifty-three years. The Woodens had one son, James Hugh, and one daughter, Nancy Ann.

When I think of Coach Wooden, I think of a great teacher whose great wisdom can be seen in the following quotes attributed to him:

- Ability is a poor man's wealth.
- Be more concerned with your character than your reputation, because your character is what you really are, while your reputation is merely what others think you are.

- Consider the rights of others before your own feelings, and the feelings of others before your own rights.

- Do not let what you cannot do interfere with what you can do.

- It's what you learn after you know it all that counts.

- The worst thing about new books is that they keep us from reading the old ones.

- Things turn out best for the people who make the best of the way things turn out.

- You can't live a perfect day without doing something for someone who will never be able to repay you.

Source: *www.brainyquote.com*

Coach Wooden writes that he knows "of no prayer more beautiful or meaningful than the 23rd Psalm."

The Lord is my shepherd, I shall not want.
He makes me lie down in green pastures;
He leads me beside still waters;
He restores my soul.
He leads me in right paths for his name's sake.
Even though I walk through the darkest valley,
I fear no evil; for you are with me;
Your rod and your staff, they comfort me.
You prepare a table before me in the presence of mine enemies;
You anoint my head with oil; my cup overflows.
Surely goodness and mercy shall follow me all the days of my life.
And I will dwell in the house of the Lord my whole life long.

Coach Wooden also included the following anonymous verse entitled "Love":

My dear friends, we must love each other.
Love comes from God, and when we love each other,
it shows that we have been given a new life.
We are now God's children and we know Him.
God is love and anyone who doesn't love others
has never known Him.
God showed His love for us when he sent His only Son
into the world to give us life.
Real love is not our love for God, but His love for us.
God sent His Son to be like sacrifice
by which our sins are forgiven.
Let us give Him thanks.

Danny Wuerffel –
Heisman Trophy winner/U. of Florida

CollegeFootballNews.com has ranked the University of Florida's Danny Wuerffel number 37 out of their All-time Top 100 collegiate football players. That's quite an honor, but one that I will show is well-deserved.

Wuerffel led the Gators to four conference titles, two national championship games, and one national championship. He was an Academic All-American. In his career, he passed for 10,875 yards and 114 touchdowns. His career passing rating of 163.5 was the best in NCAA major college history. Moreover, he is the only college quarterback to have ever had two consecutive seasons with a passing record of over 170.

In the 1996 SEC title game against the eleventh-ranked Alabama Crimson Tide, he threw six touchdown passes. His efforts during his senior year (1996) were recognized when he was awarded the Heisman Trophy.

The only thing better than Danny Wuerffel the football player is Danny Wuerffel the man. Danny's father was an Air Force chaplain, and Danny obviously got many of his Christian principles from his dad as well as from his mom, who was also active in the church.

In 1996, Danny declined an offer to be a member of *Playboy Magazine*'s pre-season All American football team. He also passed on their offer to be named National Scholar Athlete of the Year.

Wuerffel's pro career included stints with the New Orleans, Green Bay, Chicago, and Washington teams, as well as a season with the Rhein Fire in Germany. Since his retirement, Danny and his wife Jessica have been very active with Desire Street Ministries. They are very involved in the establishment of the Desire Street Academy for boys and girls in New Orleans's inner city. Danny's task was exponentially increased in the aftermath of Hurricane Katrina when he had to find an alternate location for the school and housing for its students.

Danny and Jessica have one son, Jonah. I look forward to reading the book, *Danny Wuerffel's Tales from the Gator Swamp: Reflections of Faith and Football*. If that's a full title, it's probably because Danny has lived a very full life.

Danny sent us two prayers that are his favorites: the Lord's Prayer, which you can find printed as the favorite prayer of several other celebrities (Patty Berg, Mike Eruzione, Archie Griffin, Tom Lester, Andy Pafko, and Billy Pierce) and the beautiful Psalm 139, verses 23 and 24. I would encourage you to open your bibles and read the entire psalm, but here are the two verses Danny cited:

<u>Psalms 139:23-24</u>
Search me, O God, and know my heart:
test me, and know my thoughts:
See if there be any wicked way in me,
and lead me in the way everlasting.

Norma Larsen Zimmer – "Champagne Lady"/*The Lawrence Welk Show*

Everyone who really knows my mother-in-law, Virginia Supik, knows not to phone her between the hours of 7:00 and 8:00 on Saturday evenings. That hour is dedicated to watching the Lawrence Welk program (the only modern, contemporary program which is shown such reverence by Mom Supik is *Everybody Loves Raymond*). So I was happy to receive a prayer from none other than the "Champagne Lady" herself, Norma Zimmer.

Norma, early in her career, performed in such vocal groups as the Norman LuBoff Choir, the Pete King Chorale, and the Ken Darby Singers. She also sang backup for Frank Sinatra, Judy Garland, and Gordon Jenkins.

After she worked as a studio singer for Lawrence Welk's 1956 Thanksgiving album, she was contracted to travel with Welk's group for personal appearances for the next three years. Norma then decided to resign from such travels so that she could raise her two sons. Welk persuaded her to stay with the television act and there she became the "Champagne Lady" for the next twenty years. Her duties were to sing a solo, a duet, and often to close the program by dancing with Mr. Welk.

Her hobbies include oil painting and needlework.

Norma writes that her, "ardent prayer is to be used by God. Each morning, I thank God for another day, and pray that He will use me to be a blessing to someone that day. I pray that I will glorify Him in all that I do. When I'm weak or feel inadequate, I repeat this verse of scripture:

I can do all things through Christ which strengthens me!
(Phil. 4:13)

Prayer Quotations

*(What various historical figures have said about
the nature, power, and efficacy of prayer)*

Most people do not pray, they only beg.
George Bernard Shaw

*Prayer does not change God,
but it changes him who prays.*
Soren Kierkegaard

Don't pray when it rains if you don't pray when the sun shines.
Leroy Robert "Satchel" Paige

*The fruit of silence is prayer,
the fruit of prayer is faith,
the fruit of faith is love,
the fruit of love is service,
and the fruit of service is peace.*
Mother Teresa

Prayer is simply a two-way conversation between you and God.
Billy Graham

I do not pray for success.
I pray for faithfulness.
Mother Teresa

More things are wrought by prayer than this world dreams of.
Alfred Lord Tennyson

You pray in your distress and in your need:
would that you might pray also in the fullness of your joy
and in your days of abundance.
Kahlil Gibran

Prayer is an invisible tool which is wielded in a visible world.
Leo Tolstoy

The fewer the words, the better the prayer.
Martin Luther

A generous prayer is never presented in vain;
the petition may be refused, but the petitioner is always,
I believe, rewarded by some gracious visitation.
Robert Louis Stevenson

Do not always ask when you pray,
but instead affirm that God's blessings are being given,
and spend most of your prayers giving thanks.
Norman Vincent Peale

Prayer is not asking. It is a longing of the soul.
It is daily admission of one's weakness...
It is better in prayer to have a heart without words
than words without heart.
Mahatma Gandhi

There are thoughts which are prayers.
There are moments when, whatever the posture of the body,
the soul is on its knees.
Victor Hugo

Do not pray for easy lives. Pray to be stronger men.
John F. Kennedy

My words fly up, my thoughts remain below,
words without thoughts never to heaven go.
William Shakespeare

When the gods wish to punish us, they answer our prayers.
Oscar Wilde

I have had prayers answered—most strangely so sometimes—
but I think our Heavenly Father's loving kindness has been more
evident in what He has refused me.
Lewis Carroll

I have so much to do that I shall spend my first three hours in prayer.
Martin Luther

In souls filled with love, the desire to please God is continual prayer.
John Wesley

*I have been driven many times to my knees by the overwhelming
conviction that I had nowhere else to go. My own wisdom, and that
of all about me, seemed insufficient for the day.*
Abraham Lincoln

*The men who have guided the destiny of the United States have
found the strength for their tasks by going to their knees. This
private unity of public men to their God is an enduring source of
reassurance for the people of America.*
Lyndon B. Johnson
*Avail yourself of the greatest privilege this side of heaven.
Jesus Christ died to make this communion and communication
with the Father possible.*
Billy Graham

*We pray most when we say least,
and we may pray least when we say most.*
St. Augustine of Hippo

*Remember that you can pray anytime, anywhere.
Washing dishes, digging ditches, working in the office,
in the shop, on the athletic field, even in prison—
you can pray and know God hears!*
Billy Graham

*Pray often, for prayer is a shield to the soul, a sacrifice to God,
and a scourge for Satan.*
John Bunyan

Prayer is not overcoming God's reluctance,
but laying hold of His willingness.
Martin Luther

Prayer enlarges the heart until it is capable of containing
God's gift of Himself.
Mother Teresa

The story is told of a little guy valiantly but futilely trying to move a
heavy log to clear a pathway to his favorite hideout. His dad stood
nearby and finally asked him why he wasn't using all his strength.
The little guy assured his dad he was straining with all his might.
His dad quietly told him he was not using all his strength,
because he hadn't asked him (his dad) to help.
Zig Zigler

I care not if God is on my side; my constant hope and prayer
is that I may be found upon God's side.
Abraham Lincoln

Her eyes are homes of silent prayer.
Alfred Lord Tennyson

To get nations back on their feet,
we must first get down on our knees.
Billy Graham

Every morning lean thine arms awhile
Upon the window-sill of heaven
And gaze upon thy Lord
Then with vision in thy heart,
Turn strong to meet thy day.
Thomas Blake

What can I give Him poor as I am?
If I were a shepherd, I would give Him a lamb,
If I were a wise man, I would do my part,
But what I can I give Him,
Give my heart.
Christina G. Rossetti

If the heart wanders or is distracted, bring it back to the point quite
gently and replace it tenderly in its Master's presence. And even if you
did nothing during the whole of your hour but bring your heart back
and place it again in our Lord's presence, though it went away every
time you brought it back, your hour will be very well employed.
St. Francis de Sales

There is a place where thou canst touch the eyes
Of blinded men to instant, perfect sight;
There is a place where thou canst say, "Arise"
To dying captives, bound in chains of night;
There is a place where thou canst reach the store
Of hoarded gold and free it for the Lord;
There is a place—upon some distant shore –
Where thou canst send the worker and the Word.
Where is that secret place—dost thou ask, "Where?"
O soul, it is the secret place of prayer!
Alfred Lord Tennyson

*The Christian needs to be alone during a definite period each day
for meditation on scripture ... and for prayer ... even during
times of spiritual dryness and apathy. It matters little what form
of prayer we adopt ... or how many words we use. What matters
is the faith which lays hold on God, knowing that He knows our
needs before we even ask Him. That is what gives Christian prayer
its boundless confidence and its joyous certainty. We simply make
petitions and requests to One who has the heart of a Father. Of
course, God's will must be the primary object of our prayers ... and
we must recognize prayer as an instrument of God's will. Therefore,
we pray that God's will may be done throughout the world ... and
in intercessory prayer, we bring people ... from around the world
... into the presence of God. Every intercession potentially draws
the one for whom it is intended into a life-changing relationship
with Christ. And in intercession, I move into the other man's
place. I enter his life ...his guilt and distress. I am afflicted by his
sins and his infirmity. If .... as we pray ... we recognize our own
responsibility for the world's guilt and our own guilt in the death
of Christ ... then we can act upon and affect the lives of men and
women throughout the world.*

Dietrich Bonhofer

*To pray is to pay attention to something or someone other than
oneself. Whenever a man so concentrates his attention—on a
landscape, a poem, a geometrical problem, an idol, or the True
God—that he completely forgets his own ego and desires, he
is praying ... The primary task of the schoolteacher is to teach
children, in a secular context, the technique of prayer.*

W.H. Auden

O Lord, my God,
I have trusted in Thee;
O Jesu, my dearest One,
Now set me free.
In prison's oppression,
In sorrow's obsession,
I weary for Thee.
With sighing and crying,
Bowed down in dying,
I adore Thee, I implore Thee, set me free.
Mary Queen of Scots
(written in her book of Devotions before her execution by
Swinburne in Mary Stuart)

But maybe prayer is a road to rise,
a mountain path leading toward the skies
to assist the spirit who truly tries.
But it isn't a shibboleth, creed, nor code,
it isn't a pack horse to carry your load,
it isn't a wagon, it's only a road
And perhaps the reward of the spirit who tries
is not the goal, but the exercise!
Edmund Vance Cooke,
Prayer, The Uncommon Commoner

When the time comes, like now, then the storm around me does
not matter. Nothing human or earthly can touch me. A wilder
storm of peace gathers in my heart. What seems unpossessable, I can
possess….What is unutterable, I can utter. Because I can pray, I
can communicate. How do people endure anything on earth if they
cannot have God?
Dr. Thomas A. Dooley

Prayer for many is like a foreign land. When we go there, we go as a tourist. Like most tourists, we feel uncomfortable and out of place. Like most tourists, we therefore move on before too long and go somewhere else.
Robert McAfee Brown
(Intro to John B. Coburn's Prayer and Personal Religion, Westminster 1967)

You can do more than pray after you have prayed, but you cannot do more than pray until you have prayed.
John Bunyan

He prayeth best who loveth best all things both great and small.
Samuel Taylor Coleridge
("The Rime of the Ancient Mariner," part VII)

*Hold prayer in high esteem.
It is the foundation of all virtues,
and the source of all grace needed to sanctify
ourselves and to discharge the duties of our employment.*
St. Jean Baptiste de la Salle—adapted

He prayeth well who loveth well both man and bird and beast.
Samuel Taylor Coleridge
("The Rime of the Ancient Mariner," part VII)

And Satan trembles when he sees the weakest saint upon his knees.
William Cowpen
(Hymns –Exhortations to Prayer)

A good deed is the best prayer.
Robert Green Ingersoll

Take time to think,
it is the source of power.
Take time to read,
it is the foundation of wisdom.
Take time to play,
it is the secret of staying young.
Take time to be aware,
it is the opportunity to help others.
Take time to laugh,
it is the music of the soul.
Take time to be friendly,
it is the road to happiness.
Take time to dream,
it is what the future is made of.
Take time to pray,
it is the greatest power on earth.
Unknown English Author
(adapted from Eccl. 3:1)

DENNIS THE MENACE

"I'LL TALK TO YOU TOMORROW NIGHT, SAME TIME, SAME PLACE...AMEN."

Amen.

Readers may want to become involved with Chuck Spinner's next project. Many grandparents have heart-warming and/or humorous stories involving interactions with their grandchildren. To share one or more of these touching incidents with other readers, please send these accounts to: Chuck Spinner, P.O. Box 406, Ashville, New York 14710-0406. Please indicate the names and ages of the grandchildren at the time of these occurrences. Whether an individual story is published is up to the discretion of Mr. Spinner and his publisher. Know that these stories cannot be returned, may be adapted and changed to suit the needs of the editor, and cannot be given remuneration other than the satisfaction of sharing and preserving one's precious memories in this type of publication. Please copy this page. By signing and returning this page with the story of your grandchildren, you agree to have your story printed in Mr. Spinner's book and you agree also to the terms and conditions listed above. Thank you!

Signature: _____

Address: _____

_____

Date: _____